Kim Gordon

Is It My Body? Selected Texts

Institut für Kunstkritik
Frankfurt am Main
Isabelle Graw
Daniel Birnbaum

Kim Gordon

Is It My Body? Selected Texts

Edited by Branden W. Joseph

Sternberg Press

Preface

Isabelle Graw, Daniel Birnbaum

When we founded the Institut für Kunstkritik a decade ago, it was our ambition to involve not only the leading critics and art historians of our time, but also artists whose practice involves critical texts. Kim Gordon is such an artist. And beyond that, she is a role model and a great source of inspiration for generations of artists, musicians, and writers who believe in the necessity of transcending disciplines. For us, this book represents a dream come true.

"Paradoxically, her [visual] art is the least well known of her activities," as Matthew Higgs stated, the curator of Gordon's recent retrospective at White Columns in New York. "Yet it's at the root of everything she does." Her real academy, she explains in a conversation with Jutta Koether conducted for this volume, was Dan Graham, who made clear that it wasn't quite enough to make art and show it in a gallery. Instead, you ought to be part of a conversation beyond your discipline, "a more widespread and interesting cultural dialogue." That is exactly what this volume of texts represents. We want to thank its devoted editor, Branden Joseph, for his brilliant work, and Kim Gordon for letting us publish her texts in our series. This book, we believe, will become an instant classic.

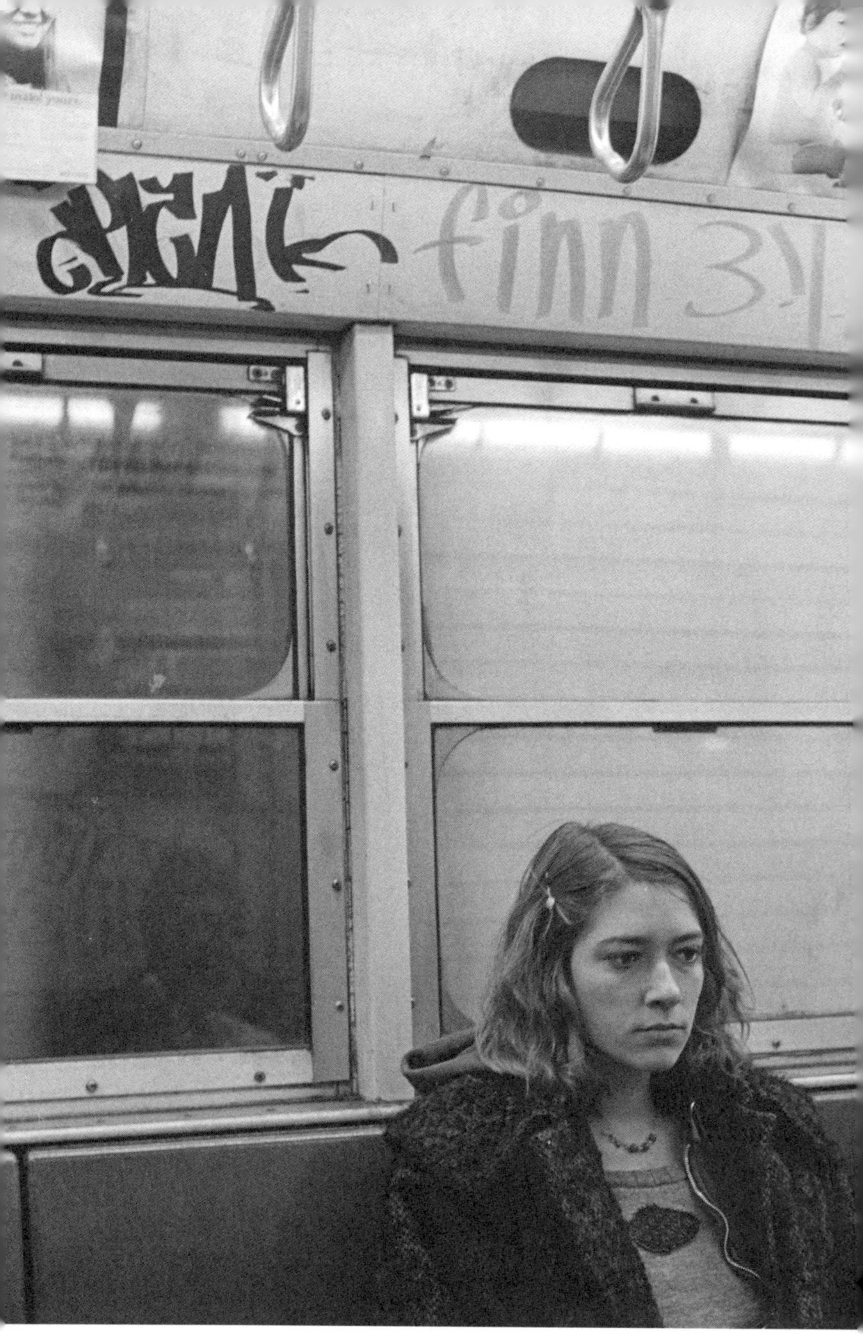
finn

Introduction
Branden W. Joseph

The relationship of Kim Gordon's band Sonic Youth to the New York art scene of the 1980s and '90s has become canonic enough to have inspired a number of museum exhibitions.[1] Even so, her writings from the time remain surprisingly overlooked. Often appearing in the guise of straightforward, unadorned prose, Gordon's texts, like those of the more celebrated artist-writers of her generation—Barbara Kruger, John Miller, Mike Kelley, and Dan Graham (all of whom Gordon published alongside)—prove subtle, insightful, and rewarding of repeated scrutiny.

Ranging from stand-alone neo-Conceptual artworks to wide-ranging cultural analyses to tour diaries and interviews, the writings collected in this volume chart Gordon's trajectory from art student to practicing artist to member of one of the most influential rock groups of our time. Yet, while approachable on that level, they ultimately prove more compelling—and justify their inclusion in the Institut für Kunstkritik series—for their contribution to the discourse surrounding art, architecture, film, fashion, and rock music that catalyzed art scenes from New York to Los Angeles, Toronto, London, and Cologne at the end of the twentieth century. Although frequently gravitating to rock and roll and interior design, and the manner in which the two come together in music clubs (most notably in "Making the Nature Scene," 1983), Gordon's reflections always

1 See for instance the traveling exhibition "Sonic Youth etc.: Sensational Fix," organized by LiFE, Saint-Nazaire, France, 2008; and "NYC 1993: Experimental Jet Set, Trash and No Star," at the New Museum, New York, 2013.

Left: Kim Gordon in New York, ca. 1975

cast a critical eye toward key stakes within contemporary art, whether the revival of Pop-art strategies, the persistence of formalist modernism, or the vicissitudes of institutional critique. Conversely, when discussing visual artists such as Kelley, John Knight, Jeff Wall, Robert Longo, or Raymond Pettibon, Gordon pays particular attention to the manner in which their work, as she puts it in "Turning the Conversation," "becomes aligned with other orders." These might be the urban, architectural, or commercial environment, the technological infrastructure, or competing realms of cultural and subcultural production.

Already as early as 1977, in the four pieces entitled "Proposal for a Story," originally presented as an artwork on 35 mm slides, Gordon contrasts the deadpan, descriptive language of Conceptual art with borderline-lurid encapsulations of television programming appropriated from popular sources such as *TV Guide*. Although lacking any visual component whatsoever, "Proposal for a Story [II]" in particular evinces a sensibility akin to what Douglas Crimp attributed that same year to artists of the "Pictures" generation such as Longo and Sherrie Levine: the "imperative to understand the picture itself"—or, in Gordon's case, the description of made-for-TV motion pictures—"not in order to recover a lost reality, but to determine how a picture becomes a signifying structure of its own accord."[2]

Throughout the early '80s Gordon continued to investigate appropriation in "Cosmopolitan Girls," "The Bedroom Displays Itself ...," "Honeymoon Habit," and, somewhat differently, the magazine piece "Men at Work." "The Bedroom Displays Itself ..." and "Honeymoon Habit" relate to Gordon's project Design Office, a faux neo-Conceptual design firm founded with Vikky Alexander to intervene in the interior decor of domestic and institutional spaces. Design Office would be recognized by both Dan Graham (who mentions Gordon and Alexander in the essay “Signs”)[3] and the Canadian art collective General Idea, who featured Gordon’s intervention in Graham’s Lower East Side apartment (in “The Bedroom Displays Itself …”) in their détournement of mass media, *FILE* magazine. “Kim Gordon’s interiors are to interior design,” they noted, “as *FILE* is to *LIFE* [magazine].”[4]

“Cosmopolitan Girls” also appeared in *FILE*. Coupling the transcription of an ad for *Cosmopolitan* women’s magazine with lyrics from Bruce Channel’s “Hey! Baby” (1961), the Doors’ “Hello, I Love You” (1968), and the chorus to the Chiffons’ “He’s So Fine” (1963), the song had been written for the short-lived girl group CKM (named after the first initials of its members: Christine Hahn, Gordon, and Stanton Miranda, aka Miranda Stanton). CKM formed in 1980 to take part in a performance arranged by Graham at the Massachusetts College of Art and Design. Graham had already begun to investigate the role of women and gender in rock music, an interest that culminated in the essays “New Wave Rock and the Feminine” and “McLaren’s Children,” as well as the influential video *Rock My Religion* (1982–84), in which he credits Gordon for “important ideas.”[5] Many, if not all, of Gordon’s critical essays draw upon and respond to Graham. The discussion of masculinity that runs throughout “Trash Drugs and Male Bonding” (a detailed account of a Rhys Chatham concert from 1980), “‘I’m Really Scared When I Kill in My Dreams,’” and “Unresolved Desires” (both 1983) forms the lesser-known half of a lively dialogue with Graham’s considerations of femininity.

2 Douglas Crimp, *Pictures* (New York: Artists Space, 1977), 3.
3 Dan Graham, “Signs,” *Artforum* 19, no. 8 (April 1981): 40.
4 General Idea, in *FILE* 4, no. 3 (Summer 1980): 15.

(Indeed, Graham's "New Wave Rock" opens with a quote from "Trash Drugs.")

As Kodwo Eshun argues apropos *Rock My Religion*, Graham approached subjects such as hippies, teenagers, and rock stars from an almost ethnographic perspective: "These are always ideal types: functional, generalised, essentialised, mythopoetic, belonging to the cultural imaginary."[6] Gordon's investigations of masculinity, including modes of identification, rituals of male bonding, and performances of gender ambiguity (by Andy Warhol, David Bowie, and Alice Cooper) betray a similarly willfully ethnographic approach. This seems to be particularly the case in "Unresolved Desires," which so exoticizes male sexuality as to denaturalize and estrange it.

Gordon also draws upon Graham's pioneering analyses of early punk bands like Devo, the Ramones, and the Sex Pistols. Citing artist and critic Donald Judd's discussion of Roy Lichtenstein's painting as "a representation of a representation," Graham asserted that punk's cartoon-like invocations of violence, fascism, and bondage adapted Pop art's ironic strategies of appropriation and self-packaging to instigate a two-fold reception: a straightforward, "popular or vernacular" reading (which takes them at face value) and a second, more distanced or abstract one that functions as a meta-commentary by placing those attributes in quotes.[7] "By expressing disgust for, or satirically deflating, liberal society's repression of (its own) vio-

5 Dan Graham, "New Wave Rock and the Feminine" (1980–82) and "McLaren's Children" (1981–82), in Dan Graham, *Rock My Religion: Writings and Art Projects, 1965–1990*, ed. Brian Wallis (Cambridge, MA: MIT Press, 1993), 116–37, 142–61.

6 Kodwo Eshun, *Dan Graham: Rock My Religion* (London: Afterall, 2012), 79.

7 Dan Graham, "Information" (1967–69), in *Rock My Religion*, 28–29; and Dan Graham, "Punk as Propaganda" (1979), in *Rock My Religion*, 99.

lence," Graham argues, "punk became associated in the media with the violence it was desublimating. The media accepted at face value punk's images of social violence because it wasn't neutralized by conventional forms of representation. What the media didn't see was that punk was *representing the representation*."[8] Gordon refers to Graham's discussions of pop and punk on more than one occasion. However, her position on art/music "crossovers" ultimately differs from his, as it does from Kelley's ascription of near-Brechtian aesthetics to Iggy Pop of the Stooges or John Miller's investigation of the commodity function in country music.[9]

Gordon develops a critical leitmotif around "impurity." This first appears in the epigraph to "Trash Drugs," taken from Dane Rudhyar's *The Pulse of Life: New Dynamics in Astrology*, which described the role of "technique" in rendering a "worker a 'pure' agent of production." In the book, Rudhyar's statement forms part of a longer discussion and definition of purity. "For water to be 'pure water,'" writes Rudhyar, "means to be water without any sediment, dirt or organic substances such as microbes and the like. It is to be *nothing but* what the chemist describes by the formula H_2O. Likewise, for a man to be 'pure' is to be 'nothing but' what he is inherently and by the right of his own individual destiny."[10] The slightly larger context of Gordon's quotation from Rudhyar reveals it to be an oblique, but nonetheless pointed reference to modernist aesthetics.

8 Dan Graham, "The End of Liberalism" (1981–82), in *Rock My Religion*, 77.

9 Mike Kelley, "Some Aesthetic High Points" (1991), in Mike Kelley, *Minor Histories: Statements, Conversations, Proposals*, ed. John C. Welchman (Cambridge, MA: MIT Press), 40–48; and John Miller, "The Commodity as a Country Music Theme" (1985), in *The Ruin of Exchange and Other Writings on Art*, ed. Alexander Alberro (Zurich: JRP|Ringier, 2012), 143–53.

10 Dane Rudhyar, *The Pulse of Life: New Dynamics in Astrology* (Philadelphia: David McKay Company, 1943), 67.

As famously argued by Clement Greenberg, who inadvertently echoed the French astrologer (and modernist composer) Rudhyar, the goal of a self-critical modernism "became to eliminate from the specific effects of each art any and every effect that might conceivably be borrowed from or by the medium of any other art. Thus would each art be rendered 'pure,' and in its 'purity' find the guarantee of its standards of quality as well as of its independence."[11]

Gordon finds a more visceral and exciting counter-aesthetic in Rhys Chatham's music, which embraces impurity on several levels: the discordant tuning of the guitars, the mixing of musical idioms (jazz, blues, rock, improv), the idiosyncratic and imperfect playing of the musicians, and the use of "cheap drugs" (Locker Room, an amyl-nitrate popper) to foster more self-indulgent performances. Eschewing the sterility of classical music style (even updated by new music composers such as La Monte Young, Steve Reich, and Philip Glass), Chatham's group approaches the dense, distorted tonalities of rock and roll, playing with and off of one another in a tense, embodied, and intersubjective manner that opens the way, ultimately, for desire. This, for Gordon, seems to be the promise of an immanent, real-time "technique" that admits "an impurity for the expression of purer [but still not completely pure!] moments."

Gordon proves a gifted phenomenologist of musical performance and an adept analyst of the manner in which the typical rock star, as "entertainment," fulfills the commodity's role in (illusorily) sustaining the audience's wish for an experience of

11 Clement Greenberg, "Modernist Painting" (1960), in Clement Greenberg, *The Collected Essays and Criticism*, vol. 4, *Modernism with a Vengeance, 1957–1969*, ed. John O'Brian (Chicago: University of Chicago Press, 1993), 86.

sexual and emotional authenticity by which to escape the actual inequities, compromises, and contradictions of their social existence. In "'I'm Really Scared When I Kill in My Dreams'" (the title is taken from the 1978 Theoretical Girls' song "You Got Me"), Gordon reflects on Public Image Ltd (PiL), Laurie Anderson, and Glenn Branca, performers who destabilize the conventional rock star's role by operating simultaneously within artistic and musical frames of reference. Gordon sees them self-reflexively incorporating certain technological, environmental, and/or contextual factors that determine the reception of their performances, similar to the design-based institutional-critique practices by John Knight she analyzed in "Turning the Conversation" (1984). Her analysis of Branca is the most extensive and developed, postulating that his concerts foreground and cause the audience to confront actually existing social hierarchies and power relations (the reason experimental composer John Cage called his music "evil").

In "American Prayers" (1985), Gordon's discussion of cult leader Charles Manson—whom she provocatively (and presciently) proposed as the model for a generation of Southern California artists—relates to that of Branca.[12] Setting Manson against Warhol as the two iconic figures of the '60s, she describes how Manson testified to the wider domains of social violence and political repression that represented the underside of '60s utopian dreams. This is the significance of Manson's "My father is the jailhouse" speech, wherein he indicted the social and political conditioning of himself and his followers. According to Gordon, an artist like Raymond

12 Manson's role would be canonized in the exhibition "Helter Skelter: L.A. Art in the 1990s," organized by Paul Schimmel for the Los Angeles Museum of Contemporary Art in 1992.

Pettibon could only engage with such material because he had more than one foot in the DIY subculture of Southern California hardcore punk. Pettibon's repeated invocations of the Manson Family do not endorse or advocate what they stand for (cult indoctrination, sexual degradation, and mass murder), but point instead to those forms of indoctrination, degradation, and repression (akin to soul murder) characterizing life in contemporary suburban Los Angeles. In this, Pettibon's attitude resembles that of Poly Styrene of the band X-Ray Spex when singing "Oh Bondage Up Yours!" (1977): "When people see people wearing bondage they think they're for bondage—but they're not. Because by wearing it or singing about it, you're against it. You don't pretend that you're not chained up and everything. You admit that you're repressed."[13]

In "Death and Transfiguration," an essay devoted to the artist Paul Thek, Mike Kelley reiterated Gordon's comparison of Manson and Warhol. Pointing to the edgier street culture often depicted in Warhol's cinema, Kelley asks why the Pop artist "never produce[d] a portrait of Charles Manson, who seems such an obvious and correct choice? What other figure so perfectly embodies the cultural conflict of the period? The answer is that there was no room for art in such a figure. To drag such base material into the hushed world of painting would run the risk of having Warhol's whole enterprise cast in a dangerous, 'low' light."[14] Like Kelley, Gordon also understood Manson to be unassimilable as an art-world subject due to him representing the low, dirty underside of the '60s. However, for Gordon, Manson's discursiveness is as significant

13 Quoted in Graham, "New Wave Rock," 121.

14 Mike Kelley, "Death and Transfiguration" (1992), in Mike Kelley, *Foul Perfection: Essays and Criticism*, ed. John C. Welchman (Cambridge, MA: MIT Press, 2003), 142.

as his dystopianism: "Manson is too articulate, too much a twister of language, too effective, to be put up as an emblem of American culture." No matter how twisted, Manson's eloquence associates him with the literary tradition of Edgar Allan Poe, Mark Twain, and Herman Melville, a legacy to which Gordon assimilates both the Southern California punk groups whose lyrics she quotes at length and the Los Angeles-based artists whose work she analyzes. The ability of such discursive practices to confront the complexities and contradictions of history (rather than merely gloss its nostalgic surface) is, on the level of content, akin to what Gordon lauded in "Trash Drugs" on the level of form: a layered, multifaceted, conflictual—and thus "impure"—signification as against the reductive formal purity that unites high art with entertainment and corporate design.

The last three texts in this collection—"Boys Are Smelly: Sonic Youth Tour Diary, '87," "Forget M/M, K/T Is the Trip," and "Is It My Body?"—were published in the late '80s and early '90s, as Sonic Youth was attaining widespread popular recognition. In them, Gordon recalls many of the same critical tropes (dominance and submission, gender and sexuality, even desublimated violence) found in her earlier writing. It is here, particularly in "Boys Are Smelly," that she muses most openly on the performance of female subjectivity, an area previously ceded almost entirely to Graham. The conversation that concludes this volume, with artist and musician Jutta Koether, a frequent collaborator of Gordon's, brings the concerns of the earlier texts up to the present. In an art world that has become ever more interested in the intersections between art, music, and design, Gordon's writings serve as an important precedent for and reminder of the critical stakes involved in thinking about such crossover production.

* * *

The texts collected in this volume have been corrected for typos and evident punctuation errors, as well as edited for consistency when needed. Wherever possible, direct quotations have also been checked and corrected. In certain instances (such as the citation of Erwin Panofsky in "Honeymoon Habit" and the first half of the C. A. Tripp quote on page 65) paraphrases seem inadvertently to have been printed as direct quotations. I have chosen not to correct them, as it would have too greatly altered the original essays' texture and meaning. In "'I'm Really Scared When I Kill in My Dreams,'" the quotation from Raoul Vaneigem's essay "Basic Banalities" was originally mistakenly cited to *Internationale Situationniste*, no. 8 (January 1963), which contains the second part of Vaneigem's essay. Portions of "Forget M/M, K/T Is the Trip" were corrected per its reprinting in Mike Kelley, *Interviews, Conversations, and Chit-Chat (1986–2004)*, edited by John C. Welchman (JRP|Ringier, 2005).

My thanks to Kim Gordon, John Miller, and the library of the Museum of Modern Art, New York, for providing copies of hard-to-find texts, to Jutta Koether for agreeing to participate in the conversation, to Max Bach for his attentive copyediting, to Katherine Abrams, Vito Acconci, Gilles Bonnecarrère, Catherine Ceresole, Rhys Chatham, Anthony Elms, Matthew Higgs, Sean Keenan, John Knight, Kathryn Kraczon, Robert Longo, Felipe Orrego, Tony Oursler, Gabriel Rodriguez, and Emily Shaw for images, and to Daniel Birnbaum and Isabelle Graw (and, of course, Kim) for their support of this project.

New York, June 2013

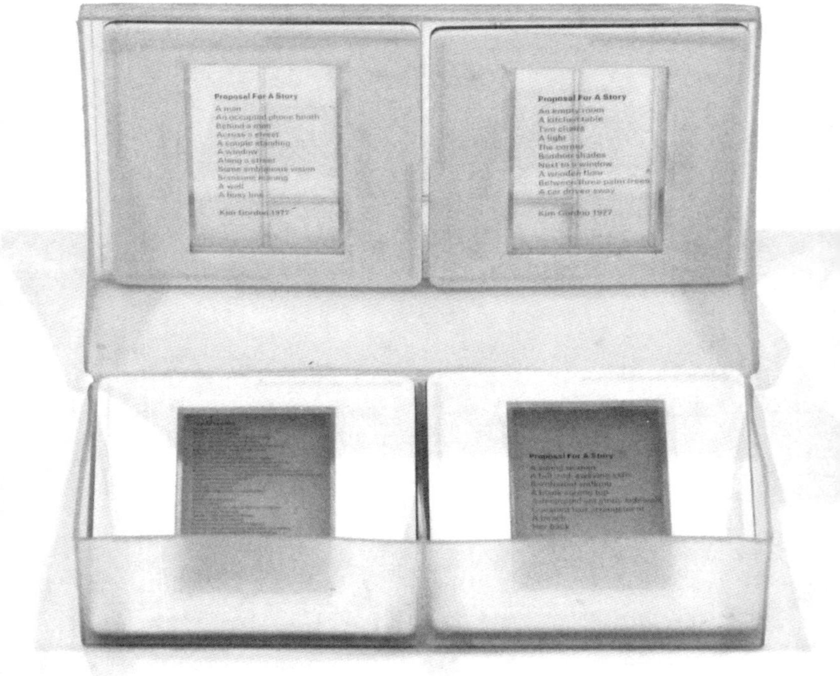
Proposal For A Story
A man
An occupied phone booth
Behind a man
Across a street
A couple standing
A window
Along a street
Some ambiguous vision
A busy line
Kim Gordon 1977
Proposal For A Story
An empty room
A kitchen table
Two chairs
A light
The corner
Bamboo shades
Next to a window
A wooden floor
Between three palm trees
A car drives away
Kim Gordon 1977
Proposal For A Story

Proposal for a Story [I]

An empty room
A kitchen table
Two chairs
A light
The corner
Bamboo shades
Next to a window
A wooden floor
Between three palm trees
A car driven away

The "Proposal for a Story" texts are reproduced as they were originally printed on 35 mm slides in 1977.

Left: Kim Gordon, *Proposal for a Story*, 1977

Proposal for a Story [II]

Stylized Italian animation
Some strong language
Violent car crashes but nobody is hurt
Some violence but make-believe
Funny-sad examination of an adult love story
Earthy language, uninhibited milieu
Subtitled anti-war satire
Violent, with touches of sadistic torture
Subtitled bittersweet Spanish civil war memoir
Grueling scenes of humans mauled by ants
Subtitled dark comedy, with elements of fantasy and satire
Adult treatment of youth coming of age, some sex and violence
Subtitled romantic tragedy
Some bathroom humor
Graphic war action
Considerable sadism and brutality
Violent
Some salty language
Violent action
Amoral, crude disrespect for law, some sex
Some strong language
Thriller, with graphic violence
Considerable bloodshed
Subtitled mature view of childhood
Considerable destruction, disrespect for police
Amoral, considerable violence and killing
Subtitled Italian comedy-drama, salty language
War recreated with gruesome fidelity
Harrowing portrayal of mental illness
Raunchy humor, fairly specific sex

Teenagers caught up in a sexual assault
Intense adult relationship
Steamy soap opera including a strong abortion scene
Violent, grueling
Grisly, shocking effects
Heavily sexual

Proposal for a Story [III]

A man
An occupied phone booth
Behind a man
Across a street
A couple standing
A window
Along a street
Some ambiguous vision
Someone leaning
A wall
A busy line

Proposal for a Story [IV]

A young woman
A full, red, swaying skirt
Barefooted walking
A black sorong top
A decorated yet stony sidewalk
Constant hair arrangement
A beach
Her back

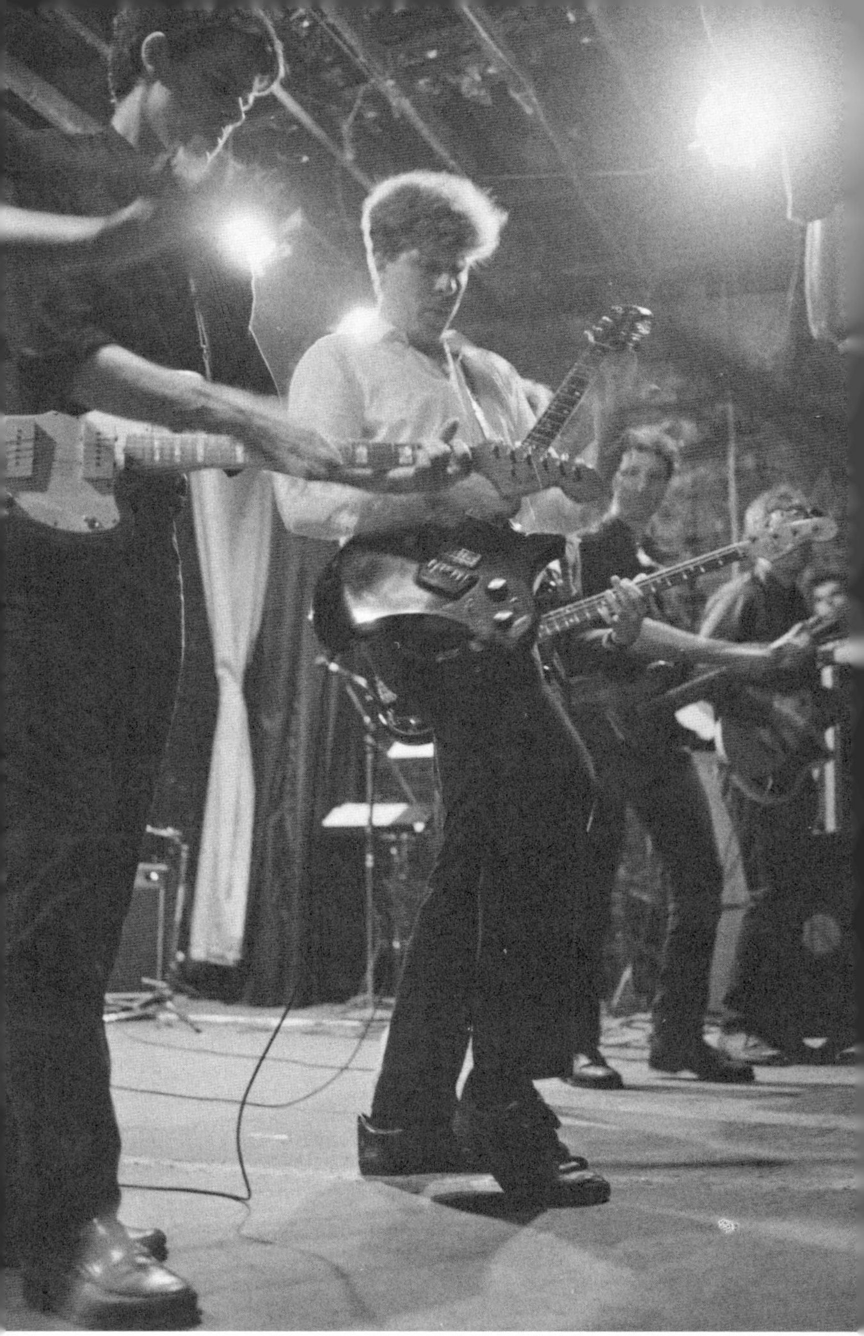

Trash Drugs and Male Bonding

> Technique means a method to eliminate all impurities which lead to waste of power; to make a worker a "pure" agent of production, without conflicts, complexes or fears.
> —Dane Rudhyar

Throughout one's life one becomes "out of tune." Four men. Three guitars, tuned discordantly, to the same key, and drums. Fifteen sections separated by alternating eight and sixteen counts strummed out by the composer, Rhys Chatham. Wearing a white dinner jacket, standing in the center, he plays for eight counts, the notes resounding like church bells, he turns with one foot forward and, holding his guitar like a weapon, looks challengingly at the audience. Cue end of prelude. Simultaneously Wharton Tiers, Robert Longo, and Jules Baptiste begin—crashing into the air and moving forward like a locomotive in somebody's wet dream. Syncopated rhythm, playing a beat every sixteen beats and then a chord every sixteen beats against Rhys's overtones, a solo which becomes a melody throughout. As Glenn Branca states in the *NY Rocker* in reference to Rhys's work, "The tones can begin bouncing so frenetically that they will seem to have no relationship to the base rhythm." The prelude returns, Rhys strokes sixteen out of tune. Jules, dressed in dark slacks, a black leather jacket, white shirt, and tie, reaches for the bottle of Locker Room and hands it to Robert, who lifts it to his nose then hands it to Rhys, who takes it while continuing to play with the other hand. Wharton, sitting in the back wearing a plaid shirt, smiles unabashed, but

Originally published in *Real Life Magazine*, no. 3 (March 1980).

Left: Rhys Chatham, 1987

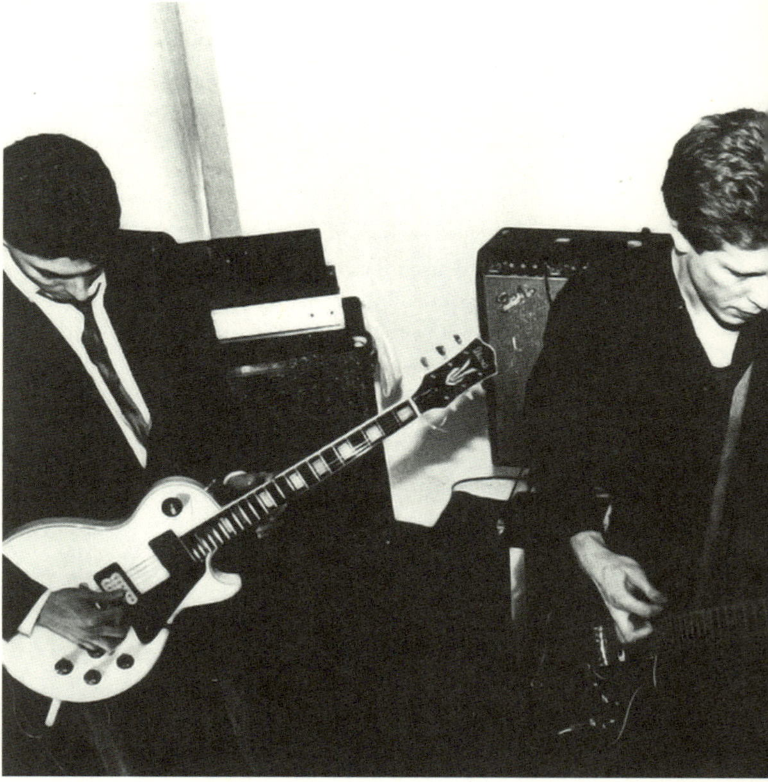

Jules Baptiste, Rhys Chatham, Wharton Tiers, and Robert Longo
performing *Guitar Trio*, ca. 1980

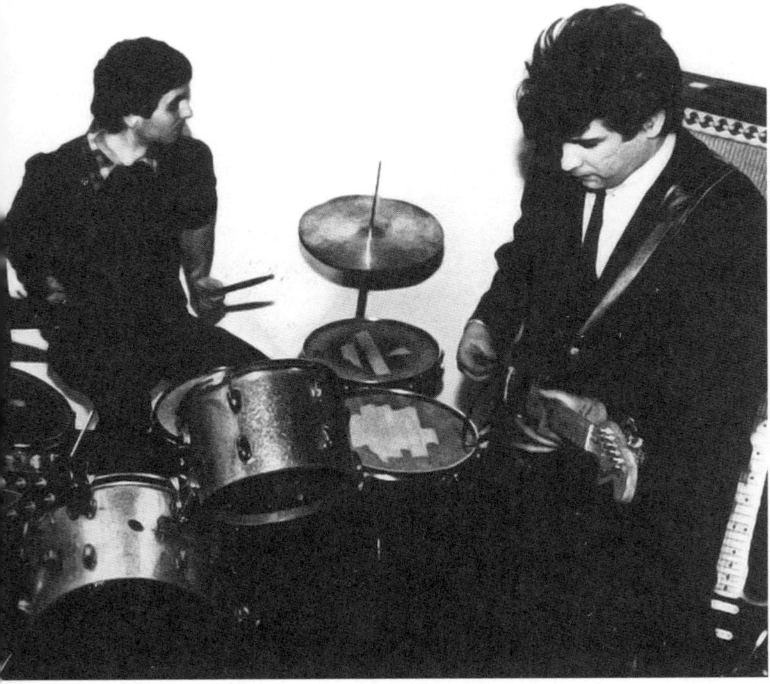

does not indulge. 1, 2, 3, 4 … The second section begins like the first, the chord becoming a little longer. Jules begins smiling over somewhere as if he were sitting in the audience. Robert is dressed in a dark suit, his guitar blends into his torso, giving the appearance of one object instead of two. He begins his solo, improvising from the preceding very deep chords rather than working with the classically based overtonal quality of Rhys's playing. In keeping with his background he plays a traditional rock bass line and turns to face the drummer, Wharton, jumping into the air to give momentum to the monumental bass lines, emphasizing the distance in the overtones and moving the music forward. For a minute Jules seems overwhelmed by the density as he watches Rhys, intently rocking back and forth towards the audience, and Robert, who seems to have taken Wharton on as a partner in crime. Jules starts his playing where you least expect it, it comes in asymmetrical, airy; rhythmic forms uncompleted. The high notes whistle, and become symmetrical to Robert's rhythm. The music builds and then Rhys, cutting it off, returns to that prelude which begins to seem like foreplay. Going into the next section the intensity is already established, the small bottle already passed around. Talking about his musicians' playing during this part, Rhys endearingly claims that they become monsters. Rhys has set the basic structure on something which is impure, a guitar out of tune. To achieve a perfection or purity of form in music is impossible because there is nothing pure about music except a style that is part of the tradition of classical music and made modern by "new music" composers such as La Monte Young, Phil Glass, and Steve Reich. Once you include the musicians as individuals a certain amount of control is given up and the music can then be allowed to be impure and potentially more exciting. It becomes more like rock music, which often relies on a particular grouping of people setting up varying tensions, timings, and tones. Cheap drugs become a means of dispelling self-consciousness in order to devote total attention to the music. Not in the way that the sensory heightened drugs of the '60s inspired the "new music" composers who were playing for a druggy audience, but the reverse. These drugs are for the musicians so they can indulge in their playing. So in a way they become the technique for the music, allowing an impurity for the expression of purer moments. Robert begins aggressively charging into Rhys in the next section. By now the sounds have become incredibly distorted, reaching a compelling density which makes it difficult to tell whether it is going backwards or forwards. The overtones set up psycho-acoustic phenomena. Some people claim to have heard male voices. The church bells return, going into the syncopated rhythm which is now louder, deeper, more gutsy. The overtone solo is more dispersed. To overcome the excitement of the previous section, the rest of the band starts back with close to the intensity achieved before the lull which reintroduced the prelude. The music continues building for a short while and then stops. Wharton, Jules, and Rhys turn and leave the stage. Robert begins playing a sort of jazz/blues improvisation. Jules comes back and, receiving the solo like a pass play, plays a rock solo. Then Wharton returns, and finally Rhys, deconstructing the music in reverse and simultaneously reconstructing it with a new attitude.

Rhys Chatham is a serious young composer who writes dirty music.

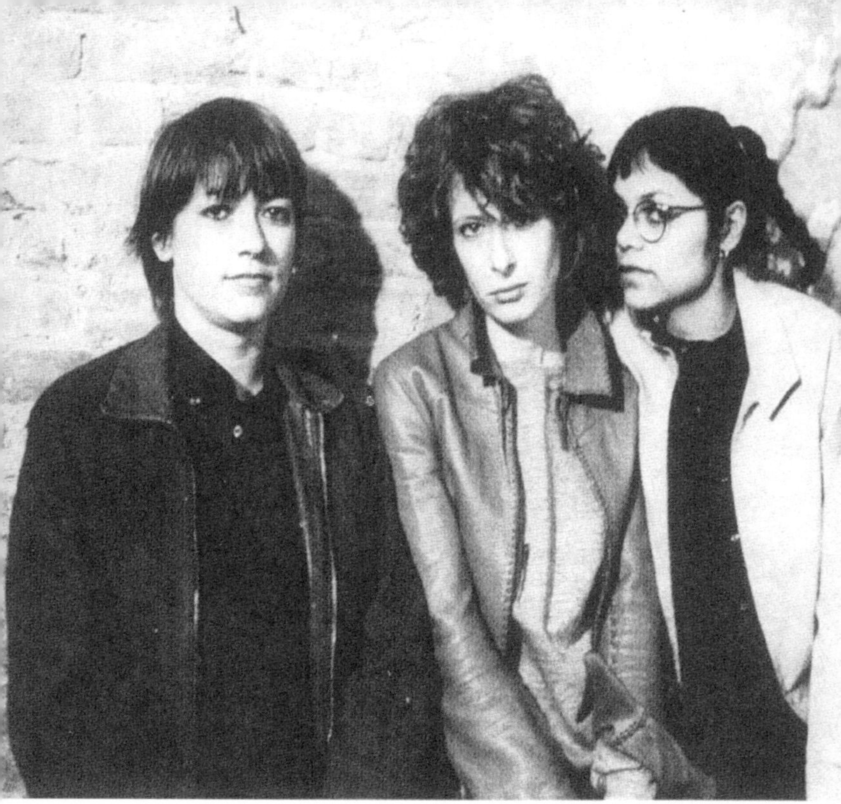

Cosmopolitan Girls

"When I hear a woman say she has finally discovered you can trust other women, I wonder just how she survived before the discovery. I've always adored my women friends. Even when a man (and it's happened to me more than once) found one of them more attractive than me, it never destroyed the relationship (sometimes I was the more attractive one). A woman breathes, loves, experiences the same as you do ... so of course she's comforting to be with. My favorite magazine says it's every bit as easy to be friends with the same sex as the opposite sex, and who else would you discuss the opposite sex with if not another woman? I love that magazine. I guess you could say that I'm that *Cosmopolitan* girl."

do lang, do lang, do lang

do lang, do lang, do lang

do lang

Lyrics by Kim Gordon and Stanton Miranda of CKM, New York City. Originally published in *FILE* 4, no. 3, "Special Global Downtown Issue!" (Summer 1980), the lyrics above are to be sung at the same time as the lyrics on the next page, ending with the chorus.

Left: CKM members Kim Gordon, Christine Hahn, and Stanton Miranda at Massachusetts College of Art, 1980

Hey, hey baby, I wanna know oh, oh if you'll be my girl

Hello, I love you, let me jump in your game
Hello, I love you, let me jump in your game

Hello, I love you, let me jump in your game
Hey, hey baby, I wanna know oh, oh if you'll be my girl
Hey, hey baby, I wanna know oh, oh if you'll be my girl
Hello, I love you, let me jump in your game
Hey, hey baby, I wanna know oh, oh if you'll be my girl

do lang, do lang, do lang

do lang, do lang, do lang

do lang

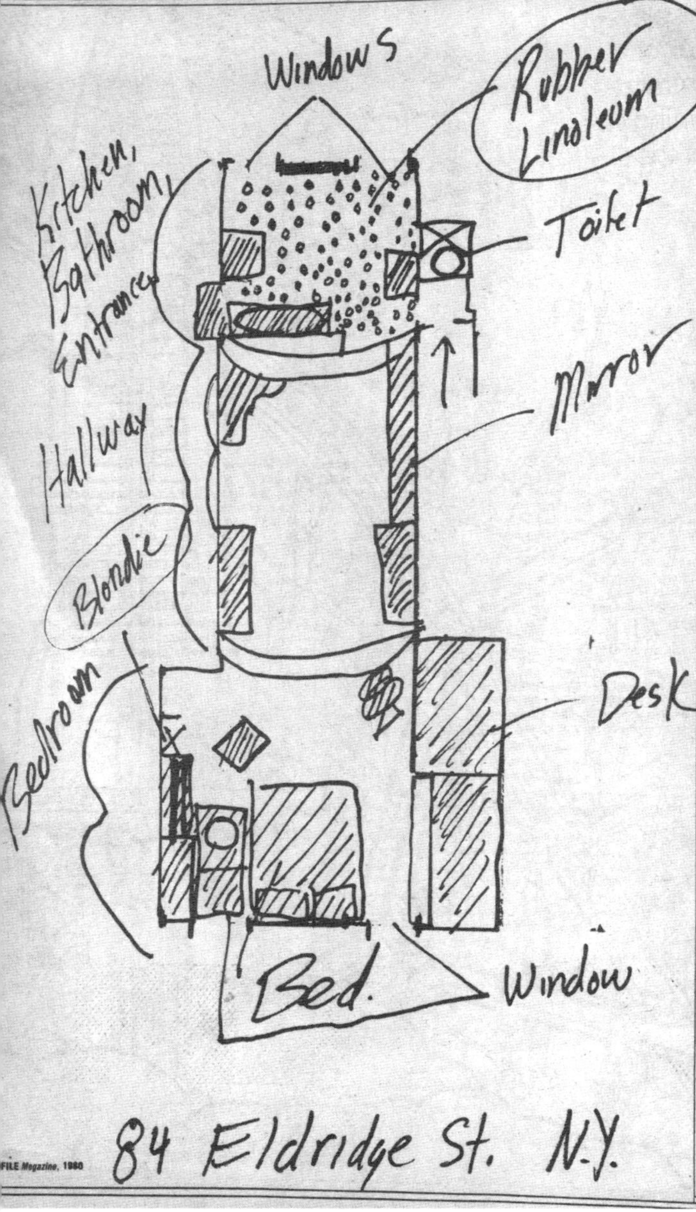

FILE Magazine, 1980

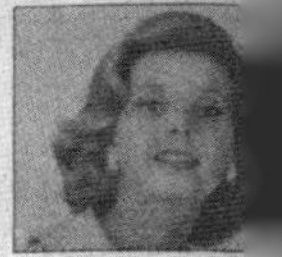

SOPHIE ENGELHAR
to sit in the den and r
the TV on and have all
on the couch with
favorite at-home past
clude cooking, read
watching "Mork and
And I like to write in r
for 20 minutes a day
walking my dogs, I rela
bath with Malmaisson
and then slip into my
loungewear – blue jea
slippers."

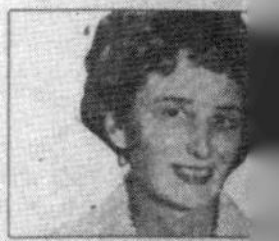

NAN KEMPNER: I love
up with a book, have a
bed and watch TV at th
time – with a fire goi
Beethoven playing . .
roll over and make love

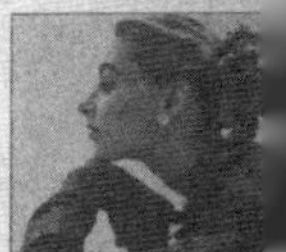

ELAINE STEINBECK:
the nights I stay home alo
luxury nights. I cook m
very good meal. I neve
make do. Often, I try ou
recipes on myself. When
home I love to wear T-
My favorites say thir
"Cronkite & Co.," whi
the guests got at W
Cronkite's birthday party
another which says "Je
Texan."

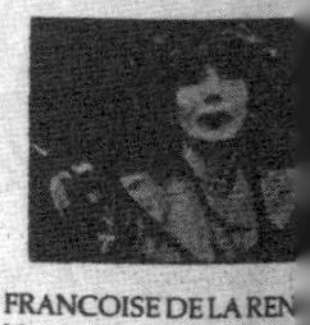

FRANCOISE DE LA REN
like to take everything of
slip on a caftan which I
with bare feet, my makeu
jewelry.

The Bedroom Displays Itself …

Enclosed is an article concerning a project I'm currently involved in thru Design Office: an experiment in collaboration concerning the interplay of Design/Architecture & Art and my position—as artist—located within these structures—hence Design Office. If you have any questions concerning this article or photos you can contact me at 515 Broadway, NY, NY 10012 / 966-7437. Kim Gordon

> "The bedroom displays itself as the center of most activity, centralized to the bed, projecting out into the middle of the room."

The client in the photograph lives in a smallish studio apartment in New York City. It is typical of all older buildings situated in and around Little Italy and the Lower East Side. The floors slope slightly to one side and metal bars cover the windows. The door to the apartment enters into the back section, containing a small stove and refrigerator, a capsule-size bathtub, and a door leading to a toilet and a skylight. The floor is tarpaper and there is a hole in the ceiling where plaster has fallen away exposing wooden boards. There are two windows that face the opposite end of the room. In between hangs a small horizontal painting at eye level. The first insertion made for the client is in this front area. Brown Pirelli tile is laid to restore the floor, covering the tarpaper. The rubber, vinyl quality being most suitable for the bathroom, kitchen, entrance room. The tile at one time was quite expensive, coming out of technological Italian chic; being no longer a new product the price has dropped, while still attaining to that look.

Originally published in *FILE* 4, no. 3, "Special Global Downtown Issue!" (Summer 1980).

Left: Original frontispiece as published in *FILE*

The color was chosen to match the rough, wooden, planks covering the other two sections of the apartment, giving the apartment that "pulled together" look.

Passing thru the arch, the middle section is narrower and longer and functions as an oversized hallway. With a large, brightly reflective, plastic material on one side and a floor-to-ceiling metal unit crammed with books. Across from this a semi-modern wooden cabinet and next to this, higher up, two small arched alcoves that are also seen reflected in the mirror which extends for more than half the length of the wall. Continuing thru the last arch, in the bedroom, there are two windows on either side of the bed that face onto the street, opposite the windows at the other end. The bedroom displays itself as the center of most activity, centralized to the bed, projecting out into the middle of the room. There is a stereo unit, a semi-monumental Sony Trinitron TV, a vivid, orange lounge chair, next to the desk another working area and another floor-to-ceiling metal unit crammed with books. Along one wall, opposite the desk are two matching white canvases, one over the other, having a black and brown hard-edge outline. Here, next to this, hanging at chest height, is the other design element added to the interior. It is a brightly painted watercolor of female rock star Debbie Harry. It is painted on 8" x 10" paper and framed on the wall in a transparent piece of plastic. The watercolor hanging below eye level becomes an ornament, enhancing the soft qualities in the apartment: the curves of the walls, the clothes hanging in the closet, and the blankets on the bed. The installation was done by the client.

Kim Gordon
Design Office
New York

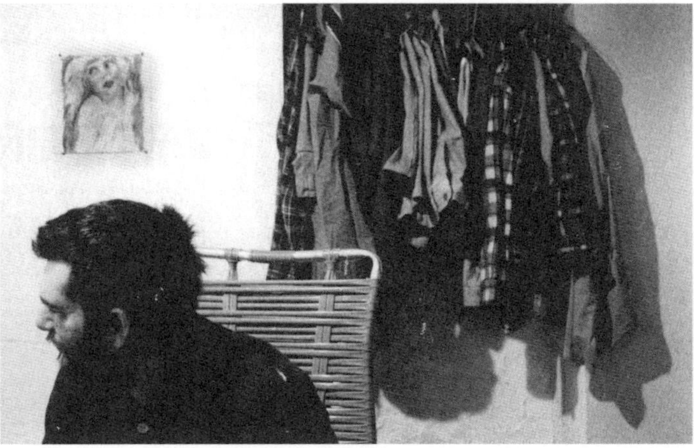

Dan Graham in his apartment after the Design Office intervention, 1980

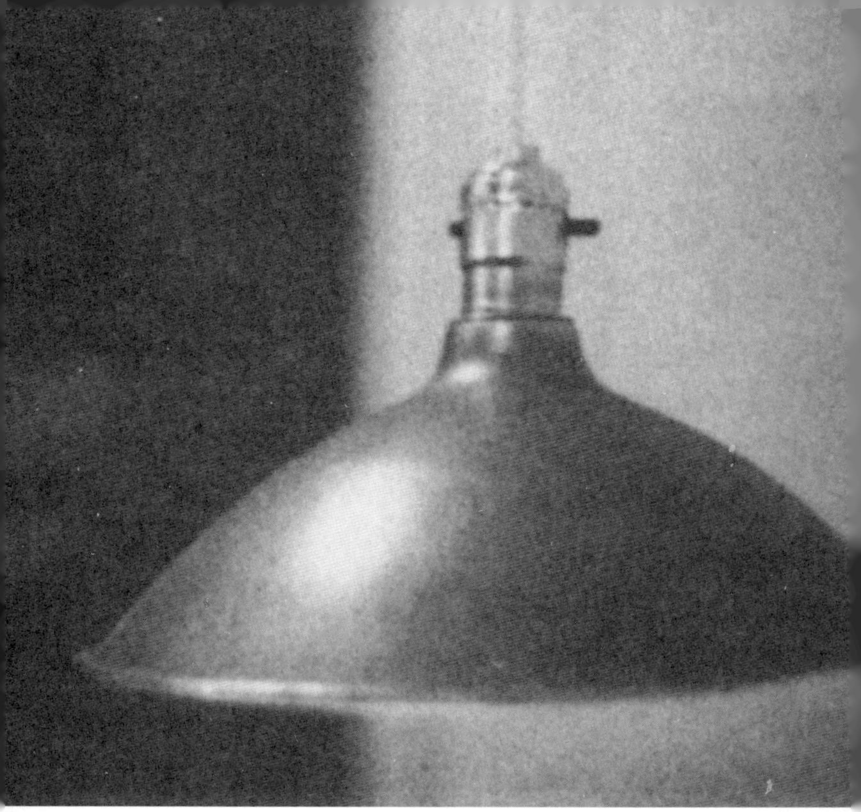

Honeymoon Habit

Your living room is the showcase of your life. A couch to carry off the dignity of the situation; Elegance revisited ... the inviting appeal of a luxuriously tufted sofa bearing the superlative upholstery skills of State Pavilion. Shown here in opulent orlon velvet with inherent easy-care characteristics. On display in design-inspiring vignettes, fully styled and accessorized. State Pavilion, Inc.
—Los Angeles Times

8 Spring Street. Clients: a couple, two musicians/artists. They both complained of lack of space; everything was too big, the refrigerator, the chair. She wanted to trade them in for smaller models. They wanted a change—but neither had the money for extensive compartmentalizing with shelves, or for furniture that was small and comfortable. They were sick of the place; it was getting on their nerves.

The rewards for success are now visible, fulfillment and the search for the Ultimate Home, all are motivating factors for our labors.
—Benita Ponderosa, Los Angeles Times

Long and rectangular, with windows at one end, the apartment is basically divided into two parts. The entrance is in the kitchen area, the place where guests are entertained. In the front, where the windows are, is a bed and a table set up for working. At one end of the mattress is a small low table, on the other side, also on the floor, a cushion chair. Hanging over the table on a long cord is a light with a metal shade, industrial looking. Back in the kitchen she explains that they want a light

Originally published in *Real Life Magazine*, no. 5 (Winter 1980).

Left: Design Office intervention, 1980

over the kitchen table so that the large floor lamp, although they like it, can be moved to make room.

Function: 1. Any ceremony, public or social gathering, or occasion. 2. The kind of activity proper to any person or thing. 3. The purpose for which something is designed or exists. A small television sits across the table on top of a metal lid covering the bathtub. On the walls are a scattering of small posters from rock events. Ornamentation: 1. Something added to enhance or improve appearance. 2. Anything or anybody that adds to the credit or glory of a group or era.

You and your faithfulness to the Elancyl Method. A simple regime. It only takes five minutes a day. It's what millions of French women use to smooth their buttocks, hips and thighs.
—Elancyl, Town & Country, July 1980

Subjectivity is a process of (history of) stability and dissolution, perpetually displacing its own positions.
—Julia Kristeva

The small mirror was spray-painted copper and placed over the stove. It was quickly moved and installed above the sink so that he could use it for shaving. Design imitates this process of self production of subjecting.

When I wear a swimsuit, I just don't swim.
—The Broadway, Los Angeles Times

Streamlining: a technological process dealing with the problem of air resistance; fast-moving vehicles. Later it became a generalized aesthetic "ideal of efficiency."
—Erwin Panofsky

A second metal shade was purchased and hung over the kitchen table. Along with the first shade, which hung in the front room, it was spray-painted copper to match the mirror.

Streamline your mind.

With the two new items added to the apartment and painted a color that is simultaneously street oriented, in a defined state, and rich looking, the project will not be resolved until the clients buy a smaller refrigerator.

Following: Kim Gordon, "Men at Work," originally published in *Cave Canem*, ed. Dan Walworth and John Miller (New York: Cave Canem Books, 1982).

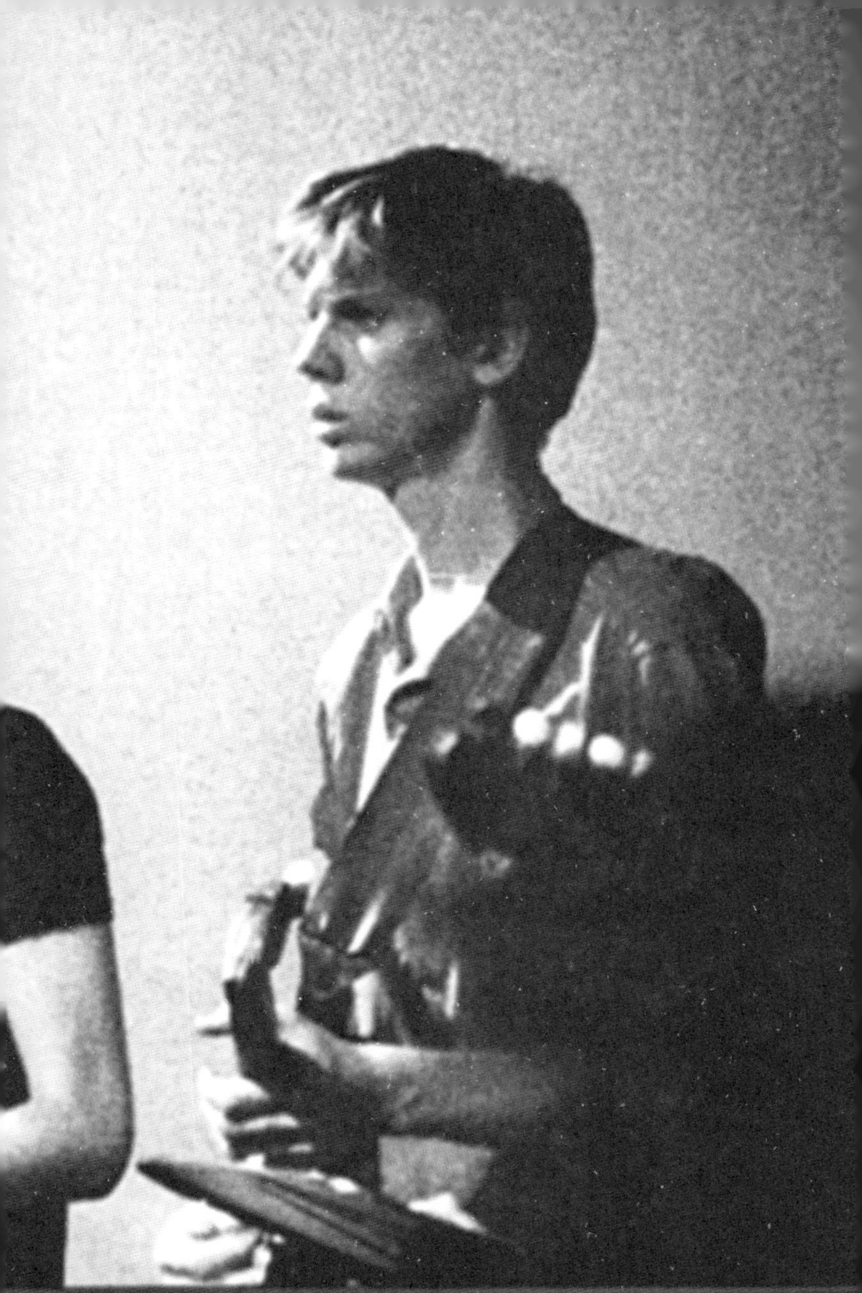

Men at Work

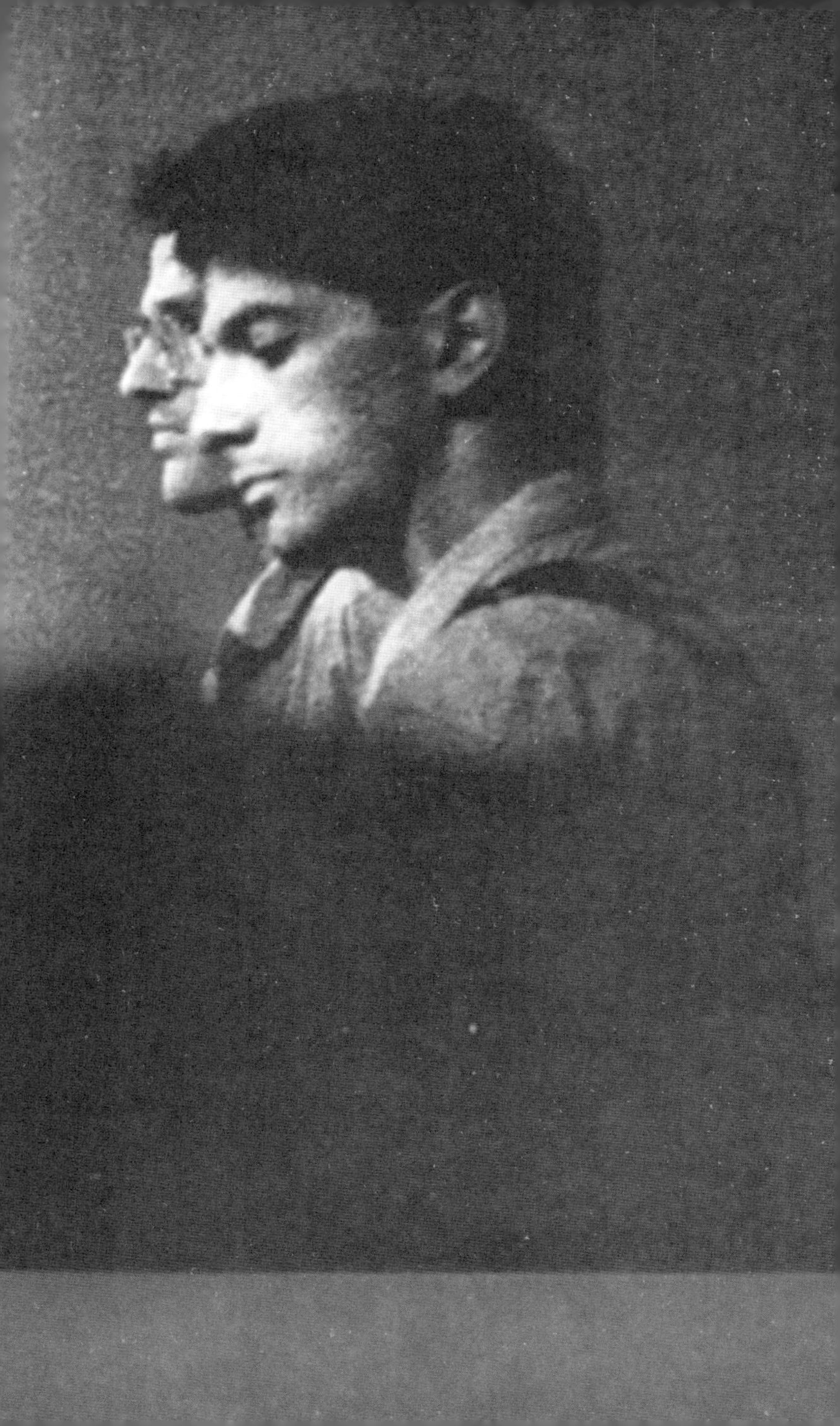

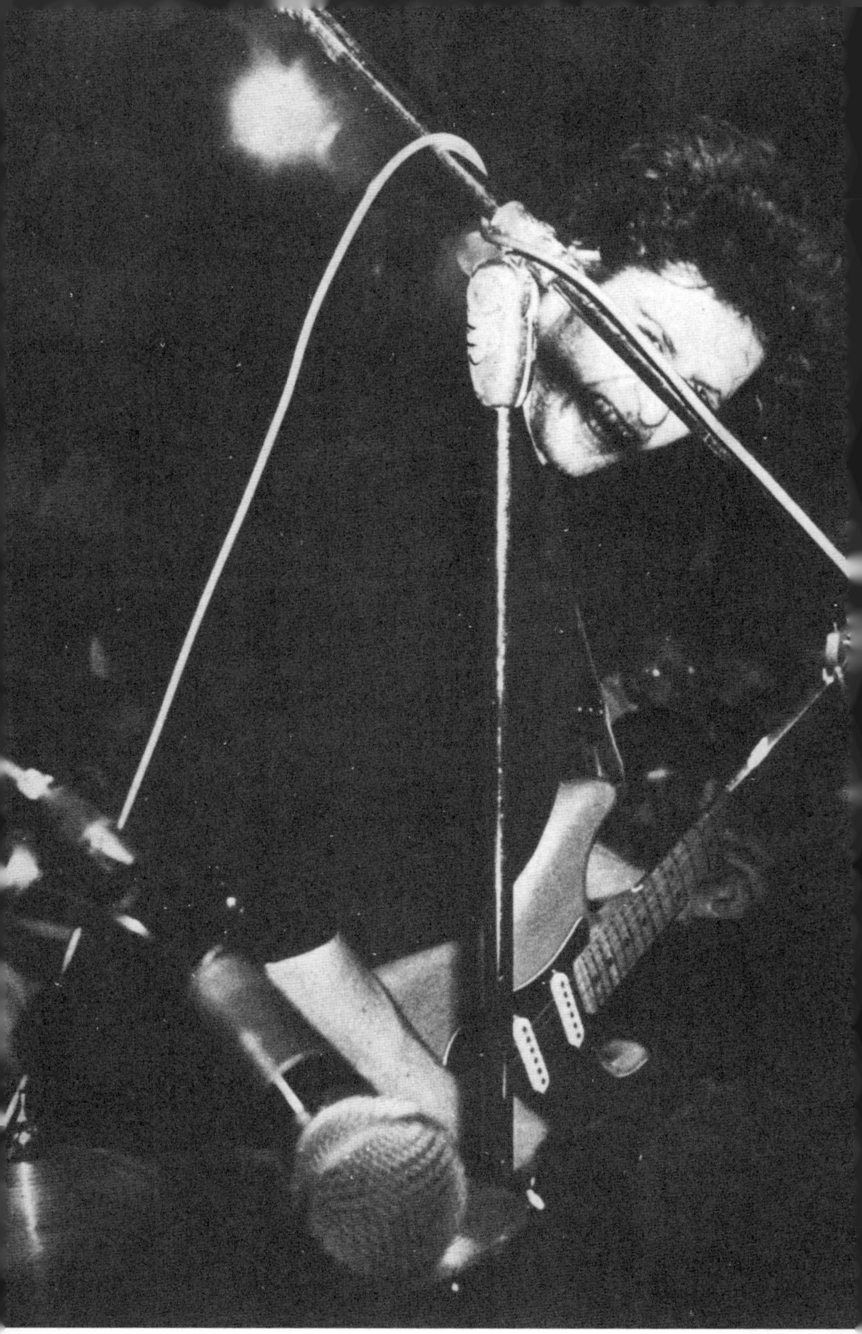

"I'm Really Scared When I Kill in My Dreams"

In the spring of 1981 the rock group Public Image Ltd (PiL) played at the Ritz in New York. That club's movie-scale video screen, which functioned as a barrier and was used to create or motivate the crowd's reaction, was the center of the performance. PiL's three members were projected on the screen, both as shadows (they were lit from behind for the video cameras) and as a video picture. A giant image of John Lydon's face, laughing, appeared, larger than the Wizard of Oz. He began singing, and then the live image was changed to a prerecorded tape of a demented commercial rock video. Furious at the ghost-like, ritualistic silhouettes of the group behind the screen—instead of, as usual, directly in front of them—the crowd constantly interrupted the music. They barraged the screen with bottles, finally tearing it down. The group hadn't intended to cause a riot; in their words, they were trying something new. They did not want to mechanistically continue in the learned role of rock entertainers. As PiL's Keith Levene remarked in an interview in *ZigZag* magazine in August 1981, "You're more honest putting on a video or sending a video round to do 30 dates, rather than sending a band around to do it. [...] You're standing up there and saying 'after you've bought my album for so many pounds and heard how great we are you can now stand in front of us and see how great we are.'" PiL has since returned to conventional rock performance.

It is almost necessary for a working rock band on the club circuit to have a booking agent and/or manager. If a club owner deals directly with the band involved, and not with a business

Originally published in *Artforum* 21, no. 5 (January 1983).

Left: Glenn Branca performing in Theoretical Girls, 1978

peer, then less money is likely to be offered. The large rock clubs in Manhattan all have basically the same policy of dealing with bands. Some of these are real showcases and some are just facades. Mailings are sent out for special evenings; these nights are not actually special, but they do give the appearance of being playgrounds for the art world, thus luring the non-art world to a supposedly chic event for which they will pay. (As in past movements of the avant-garde, these clubs appropriate the "law of assemblage" in the sense that the "real world" and the "art world" become layered.) In order to maintain an elite aura the clubs also offer their space for "art-night" parties or video and film parties which are invitational only. By constantly renovating, opening up new floors, and redecorating, each club vies for the position of "favored art club," as a yet newer alternative to the art world's alternative spaces. It seems to be what the art world wants. And on the flip side, the video/music nights at the official "alternative spaces" are designed to replicate the lounge atmosphere of the clubs, with monitors and cushions dispersed informally throughout the rooms. This symbiotic relationship has almost become a formula for a certain kind of success in both the art and the club worlds.

The club atmosphere does as little for the art that's "crossing over" as it does for the bands, and tends to subordinate the art to the place itself. Even a vision as personal as Jim Fouratt's when he did the booking at another New York club, Danceteria, can quickly turn into exploitative packaging. The support he gave American bands (with a concentration on local, New York City bands), instead of following the safer policy of booking touring English bands, actually did create an alternative club situation for a short while. His notion of art in clubs—as exemplified by this attitude toward the music—did not merely treat art as interior decoration, but allowed the art to maintain a certain integrity. The main attraction in the lounge-style clubs is a sort of skyscraper-style sexual voyeurism set up by projections, on different floors, of different eras and stylized "lifestyles."

Whereas in the club scene of the past there have been what were called "Fuck Rooms," now the atmosphere in clubs is often designed to be more one of sublimation, to the point of a sterility that has become a new sort of nonsexual eroticism. The notion of resistance—the withholding of contact between people—is a common state in current clubs. Their atmosphere designs distance—from the art, the music, other people, and oneself. The use of mirrors elaborates the already present narcissism, and individuals become spectators of themselves. Video monitors are standard design apparatus; the images are there to sustain the customers, as business dealings become mingled with fantasies—sexual, career, or otherwise. The lounge atmosphere makes the clientele feel at home or at the home of someone wealthy, creating a comfortable extravagance typical of traditional small, exclusive private clubs. The images shown on the videos are more or less unseen, and function much like televisions left on. In his discourse on the disappearance of the tragic as caused by the disappearance of the subject in art, and its subsequent reappearance, Manfredo Tafuri states, "The experience of the 'tragic' [in this century] is the experience of the metropolis. [...] The 'intensification of nervous stimulation' induced by the 'rapid crowding of changing images, the sharp discontinuity in the grasp of a single glance, and the unexpectedness of onrushing impressions,' were interpreted by [Georg] Simmel as the new conditions that generate the blasé attitude of the individual of the metropolis" (from *Architecture and Utopia: Design and Capitalist Development*, 1976). Unlike a decadent Great Gatsby lifestyle, these people all pay $5.00 to $15.00 for their pleasure and sexual entertainment. The majority of bands booked play accessible Dance-Oriented Rock.

When you're actually on the stage after dealing with the "rock 'n' roll bullshit" and noticing how the disco sound system is so much louder than the one you're playing through, you pray your instruments don't fall apart and you begin to play. You forget about everything else in the world. You forget how much the pay is and that you're not really playing for enthusiastic kids but for bored young adults—and it becomes a challenge to try to move them, blow their brains out, put some edge into the atmosphere by using what is now a technologically primitive social tool, the electric guitar.

The club is the mediator or frame through which the music is communicated. The band literally plugs into the technology of the club in order to magnify the sound, turning a possibility into actuality, making what is heard by the musicians themselves accessible to an audience. People pay to see others believe in themselves. Many people don't know whether they can experience the erotic or whether it exists only in commercials; but on stage, in the midst of rock 'n' roll, many things happen and anything can happen, whether people come as voyeurs or come to submit to the moment. As a performer you sacrifice yourself, you go through the motions and emotions of sexuality for all the people who pay to see it, to believe that it exists. The better and more convincing the performance, the more an audience can identify with the exterior involved in such an expenditure of energy. Performers appear to be submitting to the audience, but in the process they gain control of the audience's emotions. They begin to dominate the situation through the awe inspired by their total submission to it. Someone who works hard at his or her job is not going to become a "hero," but may make just enough money to be able to afford to be liberated temporarily through entertainment. A performer, however, as the hero, will be paid for being sexually uncontrolled, but will still be at the mercy of the clubs and of the way the media shapes identity. How long can someone continue to exert intensity before it becomes mannered and dishonest?

The notion of merging avant-garde and popular culture (multimedia technology) by an artist is found in its most successful form in Laurie Anderson's recent performances. The position that Anderson represents, as one who has transcended the isolation of the art world, involves a different kind of heroics from that of the rock 'n' roll persona, who represents, even if mythically, a sense of real sexuality, real life and death. Anderson's androgynous appearance and mechanical voice create an impression of organized perfection, expressing the ideal as nonsexual. She has created her own atmosphere of mastering and mimicking a technology that is usually mystifying. Wherever she performs, she accomplishes what the clubs cannot; she manipulates the audience by the unseen, creating moments that change and move along effortlessly. As in the multimedia presentations of religious organizations and corporate business, Anderson's seduction suggests, "Sit back and relax, don't think, let us do it for you, let us show you how." She is identifying with a higher order of technology-power. The technology that creates the conveniences for a certain kind of "survival" (and with that the appearances of life—eroticism, pleasure) within the commodity system is available to scientists, corporate advertising, and other commercial media, but not to artists. In an effort to attain the same degree of authority as that achieved through a technological seduction, the original intent of the art/artist is exchanged for the "other's" ends; that is, for the appropriation of people.

Elvis Presley, Eddie Cochran, Jimi Hendrix, Janis Joplin, Jim Morrison, Sid Vicious, Darby Crash, and Ian Curtis all died for our sense of "heroics," as opposed to Anderson's conceptual representation of neo-heroics. Using their egos to shape the music—in some cases believing in their media-created image and in others shaping the image themselves, whether or not they believed it—they used that image to destroy, within their own framework, the standard of what had gone before, giving rise to new forms. The audience paid to see them do this, as well as to witness the destruction of the artists' own lives—the illusory freedom becoming an actual freedom.

In whatever hellhole a performance is given, no matter how bad the world outside seems, rock music has always offered a refuge from it. Through rock, teenagers and young adults attempt to retain their purity in the face of the contradictions and compromises of the adult world. Glenn Branca, in that tradition, succeeds in turning the so-called evil, sexual power of rock music, in its primitive state, into a form of resistance. Rock 'n' roll as big business produces its own heroes through the record industry much the way movie studios created a star system. For Branca the art world offers a certain independence to pursue his work, although even within the art world the media play as important a role as they do in the commercial world. In this moment, after a few success stories of transcendence of the boundaries of an isolated art world—but before the final story—Glenn Branca is one of the most interesting figures to be "crossing over" (going back and forth, actually) from rock culture to art culture. His music reflects the dilemma of artists caught in the traditional sacrificial role of performers

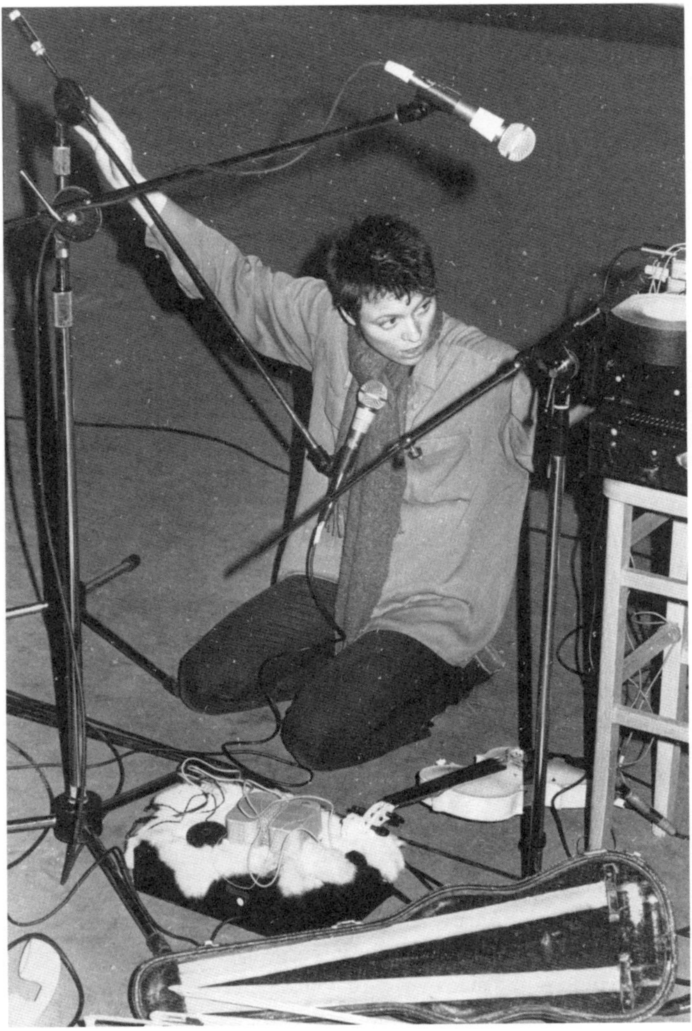

Laurie Anderson at the Institute of Contemporary Arts, London, 1981

before an audience, but extends this dilemma to include the position of the artist in relation to technology. When one views the tension between Branca's enforced closeness to mass culture and distance from it, instead of simply referring his emotionalism back to romanticism, his position becomes unique. He is a non-purist within the pure tradition of new music. Branca slips in and out of a conceptual position. The fervor and emotion in his music gives the audience, as believers, a sanctuary within a sterile pop environment, while also allowing an abstract reading. Over the last five years Branca has moved through various levels of entertainment, from a basic rock-band structure to a symphonic mode. His use of the dialectic of opposing forces of good and evil, submission and domination, yields a wide range of emotions; these shift back and forth as backdrop and foreground to an extensive range of fundamental tones and varying harmonics, which in turn create a final, intense resolution. Metaphorically this might be thought of as a kind of summoning of gods to earth in times of need.

After moving to New York in 1976 from Boston (where he was involved in theater), Branca met Jeffrey Lohn. Together they formed Theoretical Girls. As were many of their contemporaries, the two had basically been inspired by the emergent punk scene, the localized "No Wave" bands. It is well known that many of the people involved in No Wave had gone to art schools. Their involvement in music, spurred on by the cynical, anarchistic aspects of punk rock, was an alternative to alignment with the art world. Ironically, the art world in turn wanted to embrace the movement (as it seems to want to incorporate all things outside itself—especially phenomena from outside the mainstream of popular culture, such as graffiti art, rap music, or break dancing). When Brian Eno produced the *No New York* LP he brought No Wave, and specifically the bands on the record, a lot of attention; this effectively put an end to the movement because it singled out the four bands on the compilation as the definitive No Wave, causing bad feelings all around.

From the No Wave days: James Chance has gone on to achieve a certain amount of commercial success in Europe. Lydia Lunch has been through a number of band situations and musical genres; her notoriety has been based upon the persona she developed during the *No New York* days with Teenage Jesus and the Jerks and later with the more commercially acceptable 8-Eyed Spy. Recently she has been performing with various members of other groups. DNA survived and flourished as true exponents who never failed to deliver—but have recently split up. By New York standards, Pat Place has achieved commercial success within the Bush Tetras. Adele Bertei formed the Bloods, a critically acclaimed, straight-ahead R&B group. Jeffrey Lohn, ex-Theoretical Girl, has been composing and performing his own classical pieces. Margaret DeWys, another ex-Theoretical Girl, has been composing formal music. Nina Canal, ex-Gynecologist, is living and playing with Ut in England. Miranda, an ex-member of Arsenal, is recording music under the name Thick Pigeon for the Belgium-based record label Les Disques du Crépuscule. Rhys Chatham, another Arsenal graduate, has been performing "loud guitar" pieces under a variety of different band names. Paul McMahon presents a solo music/performance act. Wharton Tiers has formed Glorious Strangers. Barbara Ess has formed Listen to the Animal, and Christine Hahn plays drums with the Berlin-based Malaria. Mark Cunningham and China Burg, from Mars, have formed Don King, while Rudolph Grey, who performed with Red Transistor, now works under his own name, collaborating with various musicians.

In 1978 Branca went on to form the Static with Barbara Ess and Christine Hahn. Here he began to discover the structures of sound on which much of his current music is based. The music he made with the Static may have been his most theatrical and radical. My notes from that time read:

> They begin to play; both women have their eyes stuck to him [Branca]. Suddenly he takes off his guitar and begins to writhe on the floor covering his face and body with the dirt. The women continue to play, very cool, as he rises to the side, looks into a mirror, and proceeds to pop blackheads from his face. He returns to his guitar and joins Barbara and Christine. Barbara's and Glenn's voices stagger over each other. "It's not over, just the beginning. It's not over, just the beginning." The music climbs melodically and challenges itself with deadpan stops and jarring single beats from the bass drum. Starting slow and ending fast, sometimes just winding itself out, the lyrics more like film dialogue. The man: "Breathe in Breathe out." The woman: "Inspirez ... Expirez." Spoken in softness against the heartbeat (bass drum). Then the guitar starts its upward progression, winding in-out of the driving bass. Christine hasn't broken her gaze off Glenn; the drum repeats 1, 2, 3 with controlled resistance, teasingly. He says, "I can't eat ... I can't sleep." She repeats that in French. Again the music speeds up; "You're hurting me ... you're hurting me." He then falls to his knees forming a cross with his guitar to hers, up against it, playing, pressing it, holding it. He rises.

In the Static there was evidence of the highest degree of resistance between Branca and the two women, expressed in the music as tension and suspense. Branca competed with himself—rock being primarily male oriented—making it nearly impossible for the other two to keep up with the music. In this way he drove the music. The abrupt starts and stops and up-and-down interweaving speed of Branca's guitar and Ess's bass characterized the music, creating an atmosphere of high sexual tension, of frenzied contact and momentary withdrawal inducing a state of sustained expectancy.

Next Branca began to articulate his music further within the structure of an all-male band that played under Branca's name, gradually gaining support from within the art world. He would play mostly in clubs around New York rather than in art spaces—partly out of choice, partly out of necessity. At a concert given in 1980 at Irving Plaza, New York, Branca stood,

> his back to the audience, legs slightly parted, looking down at his guitar, the soft white hands picking over the notes; the small movements, if slow, would be a light caress. His eyes and body are alert, moving from one direction to another. Six men span across the stage, five guitars and one bass guitar, playing at different times higher and lower intertwining tones. Their poses shift with the music, which is muggy, then hot/cold, alluring. Legs cross and uncross, torsos twist slightly. A deep pulse beat penetrates the dissonance, the double strumming of the individual guitars is indistinguishable from each other. Isolated by their own timing, the knobs of their guitars are turned up as they lean forward into the resounding notes. Stilted and gliding by an order imposed from without … slowly, bam, bam, bam … the back of the hand swings against the neck, casually caressing it. Six men stand frontal, one beat resounds.

The movements necessary in creating certain sounds from the guitars, combined with the dirt produced by the sound system and the acoustics of the club/hall, unrefined and raw, defined the movements of Branca and the band, lending to them the same gut and pulp sensibility as that of rock 'n' roll.

Unlike Branca's earlier works, *Symphony No. 2 (The Peak of the Sacred)* shows a stunning split between the machinelike appearance of the performers and what is heard. This work was first performed last spring at St. Mark's Church in New York City. As the composer/creator, conductor/master Branca separated himself from the musicians, placing himself between them and the audience. Following his primitive and unorthodox method of conducting—one that is, however, known to the musicians, who are also basically "untrained"—the score and the performance set up the resolution. Homemade four-tiered guitars were used, allowing for a greater volume of sound and range of tone than guitars held in a conventional manner. The musicians had four guitars each placed in front of them, on which they hammered out the notes. What sounded melodic was actually derived from hitting the open strings in percussive beats. The extraordinary occurrences of sound were in sharp contrast to the workmanlike appearance of the orchestra. The music evoked a feeling of immateriality, suggesting homeless spirits in search of their lost bodies, ruled by technology. At the New Music America '82 festival in Chicago, John Cage, after having heard a piece for ten guitars by Branca for the first time, was quoted in the *Chicago Sun-Times* as saying, "Branca had me shaking. [...] I found myself responding in ways that brought me back to my ego. My feelings were disturbed. I recalled a piece composed by La Monte Young that was a recording at the highest volume of a gong scraping on cement. But there had been a change. The gong is no longer a thing but a performance group. [...] I found in

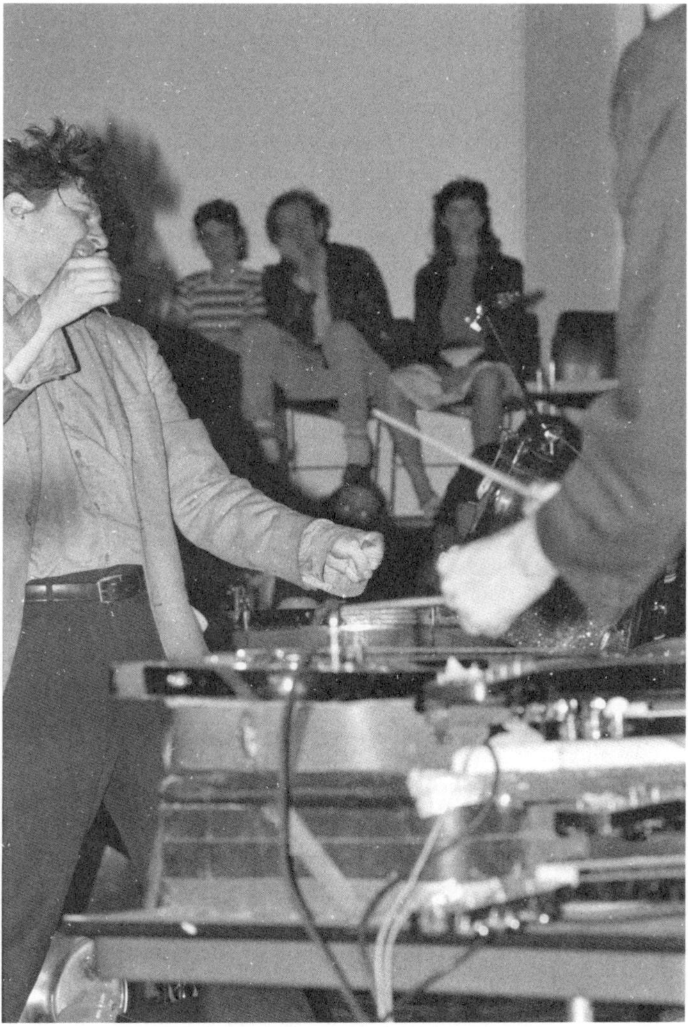

Glenn Branca performing *Symphony No. 2 (The Peak of the Sacred)*, 1982

myself the willingness to connect the music with evil—with power. I don't want such a power in my life."

Branca has placed what was once merely a reductivist formalism in a social context. He makes the audience aware of the context of "the gong" or thing, and thereby reflects the hierarchies in society. In *Symphony No. 2* the musicians represent the repressed majority—the workers who shape the object/music for their supposed later use and pleasure. Branca, as the conductor/master, composer/owner, counts on their sensitivity to, and belief in, his vision. The only musician who had apparent freedom of movement was Z'ev, the solo percussionist, who thrashed and swung his homemade instruments. Branca presented Z'ev in the role of star entertainer. Appearing in semi-bondage gear, Z'ev expressed the notion of the artist/entertainer/hero not really as master but as someone enslaved and restricted within his role, his only expression becoming one of frustration and deliverance through sacrifice. As an image of repression, he also became a representation for the majority. In "Basic Banalities," published in *Internationale Situationniste*, no. 7 (April 1962) Raoul Vaneigem writes:

> Model of gods and heroes, the master, the owner, is the true reality of Prometheus, of Christ, of all those whose spectacular sacrifice has made it possible for "the vast majority of people" to continue to sacrifice themselves to the extreme minority, to the masters. ([...] isn't the case of Christ really the sacrifice of the owner's son? If the owner can never sacrifice himself except on the level of appearance, then Christ stands for the real immolation of the owner's son when circumstances leave no other alternative. As a son he is only an owner at a very early stage of development, an embryo, little more than a dream of future ownership.)

The primitive instruments Branca uses symbolize the state of the artist within the complexity of urban technology.

Branca's latest work, *Symphony No. 3 (Gloria)*, will be premiered this month (January), and will be performed on many different instruments—some of them constructed specifically for the music. Included will be various keyboards built with resonating bars, each tuned to one or more octaves, a harmonic keyboard, motorized keyboards, mallet guitars, and harp-mallet guitars. The keyboards make it possible to move quickly and easily over a wide area of the strings; the conventional guitar involves a greater limitation. The tuning will be a reflection of the actual complex tones that make up the harmonic structure of the sound resonating from the strings. There will be little or no enharmonic distortion. This will make it possible to determine and produce specific resultant (or differential) tones. All of the instruments will be tuned directly to the intervals of the first seven octaves of the harmonic series, which constitutes 128 notes.

Branca has yet to make a record that replicates the intensity of his performances. So far there is a profound difference between a Branca record and a Branca performance. Live, his basic tool—the electric guitar—sets up a grainy atmosphere of acoustics, not electronics. His high consciousness of the visual implications of the movements required to get certain sounds means that watching the work is part of the experience of listening to it. When he threw his body around with the guitar in his earlier performances there was a sense of freedom as well as of the ever-near possibility of injury. The guitar seemed like an extension of his body. Now, with his expanding sense of music, this metaphor has extended to what has been called "an army of guitars."

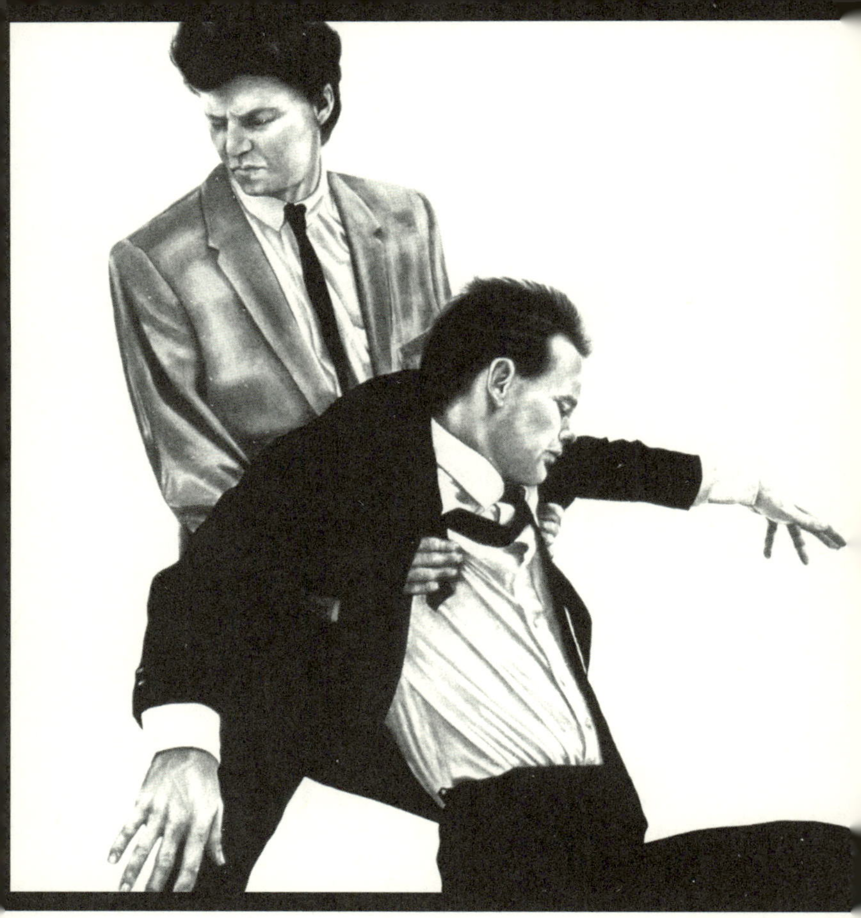

Unresolved Desires

I

> "And I invited him to sit with me. An earthangel. A streetangel. I bought him pairs of shoes! And Paris, that magnificent city of statues, glowed for me, as if lighted by heaven itself. Alas, he was a robbing angel," he sighed, feeling absently for his wristwatch. "But what had I gotten from him! Ah!" He turned heavenward. "My friend, the playwright—" He mentioned a French writer. "—was fond of saying, 'We take when we must take, and we give when we must give.' Oh, he was chic!" […]
>
> To reciprocate in any way for the money would have violated the craving for the manifestation of desire toward me. It would have compromised my needs. … The money which I got in exchange for sex was a token indication of one-way desire: that I was wanted enough to be paid for, on my own terms.
>
> —John Rechy, *City of Night*

Masculine behavior is learned through ego modeling. Boys, by the age of five, have a clear idea of those things which are "masculine," and from then till puberty, work on rejecting anything that does not fit this ideal. When they begin masturbating, they are becoming sexually aroused by eroticizing the male figure or ideal. As they go through puberty, they begin to play down male attributes for female ones because more of an identification with the opposite sex aligns them with an adult identity. The most dominant male attributes in the Western

Originally published in *ZG*, no. 7, special issue "Desire" (1983). In the table of contents, the essay is subtitled "Redefining Masculinity in Some Recent Art."

Left: Robert Longo, cover of Glenn Branca's LP *The Ascension*, 1981

world are aggression, a more actively focused sexuality, bonding with other men (male bonding), the eroticization of male attributes (hero worship), and the setting up of barriers between themselves and women (as well as with men) to retain a sense of individual male identity. Generally, as long as a man doesn't invert his role to a passive stance whilst engaging in sex with another man, he is still considered masculine.

> Certainly there is much in our society that encourages a boy to especially appreciate male qualities and male accomplishments. He is supposed to strive for these in his ego-modeling, and does, but he can also develop an intense admiration for the seemingly wondrous attainments of a usually slightly older male model, too. A high-intensity admiration very easily becomes eroticized. (C. A. Tripp, *The Homosexual Matrix*)

In Tripp's study on homosexuality, he found that societies which are "heroically" oriented have a higher rate of homosexuality. Also, what we traditionally term as a high level of virility or sexual activity (as a highly masculine trait) is found to exist prominently in the development and sustenance of sex amongst men. "A considerable body of data indicates that boys who begin masturbating early (usually before puberty) while simultaneously looking at their own genitalia can build a crucial associative connection between maleness, male genitalia, and all that is sexually valuable and exciting. […] This associative pattern sometimes manages to preempt heterosexual interests, not only by coming first but by vitalizing a nearby thought-chain most boys entertain to some extent: that since girls have no penis, they are sexless and thus sexually uninteresting."

One of the other mystiques of masculinity is the necessity for men to group together, to form a male bond. Many people claim that this is a setting for repressed homosexuality (men meeting together in club situations, like pool halls, or, in primitive societies, the barring of women from certain areas designated for men only). In Tripp's study, he found that this setting up of barriers between men and women actually had the effect of refreshing and sustaining heterosexual relationships. He claims that for any sexual motivation to prevail, "there must always be an element of tension—either through a barrier like actual segregation, or by a moral taboo. Within these male groupings, there is not enough of a gap or distance to allow for sexual arousal. [...] With hardly an exception, the most vigorously and consistently heterosexual societies are precisely the ones which use the most blatantly homosexual forms of male bonding. Here again it is as if a more or less direct expression of homosexuality (in a localized or institutionalized form) is the most effective way to satisfy it or to compartmentalize it, thus clearing the decks for heterosexuality."

These two descriptions, however, only serve to describe a certain balancing that goes on between the two sexes complementing each other even in their separation; and certainly, heterosexuality is also institutionalized as is the homosexual scene, with its own codes and barriers. One need only mention certain particularities about male bonding that might parallel what goes on in a homosexual situation, like a gay bar.

In John Rechy's book, *Rushes* (the name of a homosexual bar in which the story takes place), the narrative is a running description of the seduction and distance between men which somehow must be bridged before the night is over, and with it, the haunting tension of rejection and the excitement of an unknown coupling. He describes the distance that must be maintained until the very last moment for a sexually successful contact to be sustained, and the separate area of the room where the mystery of the atmosphere breaks down into sexual interplay. "He looks beyond the massed bodies in the main portion of the bar, beyond, toward the shrouded back. He knows that area well, as he knows every inch of the Rushes. Often after posing at the pool table, he will join the bodies beyond it. […] The sex there is not usually what Chas calls 'heavy'; more a preparation for the late-night orgy rooms."

With respect to male bonding and homosexuality, Tripp notes: "In a society where the main gathering place is a men's hut, and where homosexual relations between men and boys are prized, the boys may not be allowed in the hut at all, or they may be let in but never intimately approached there ('I'll see you in the bush tonight')."

Among homosexuals, toughness and other stereotypical male qualities are reversed and anything weak is considered effeminate and repulsive. Whether this was always true among homosexuals in our society is uncertain, but effeminacy in ancient and primitive civilization is treated as separate from homosexuality. In referring to the Greeks' depiction of sex between men in their art, Tripp says: "When they depicted an age difference between the partners, they were careful to retain the younger man's virility; they especially did not want to imply any weak receptiveness since they strongly condemned effeminacy." In other cultures they depict the receptive partner with smaller genitals.

While the '60s in our society was the era of drag queens and transvestites, they did not necessarily have homosexual tendencies. In fact, it has been found that transsexuals and transvestites have a very low sexual interest and more of an interest in themselves—their identity and self-images as women. Like other forms of identity searching and transformation that occurred in the '60s, it has reversed now in the '80s almost to a standstill. The homosexual stereotype is now flauntingly macho. Perhaps it is because many men in macho-type jobs—construction workers, policemen, etc.—are more openly homosexual? Nonetheless, they have taken on the more conservative attitudes of masculinity that the media has cultivated in the last sixty years. Advertisements for men's cologne, for example, contain more "camp" and irony than the homosexual attitudes of this era. But this is, I believe, only an indication of a more conservative attitude that is all-pervasive. "All of the men clutch their drinks—usually beer—too tightly, as if in protection against a dreaded effeminate move" (Rechy).

Inversion is a term commonly associated with homosexuality and role reversal; in its extreme form it is found in the S/M interchanges and in religious philosophies ("The meek shall inherit the earth," "Do good to those who hate you"); it encourages one to submit, masochistically, by taking on the receptive role, and also forces the partner into the other position, an act of aggression. "To dominate by submission" (Tripp).

II

> In the sixties, average types started having sex-identity problems, and some people saw a lot of their own questions about themselves being acted out by the drag queens. So then, naturally, people seemed to sort of want them around—almost as if it made them feel better because then they could say to themselves, "I may not know exactly what I am, but at least I know I'm not a drag queen." (Warhol, *POPism*)

> But then, just like drugs had come into the average person's life, sexual blurs did, too, and people began identifying a little more with drag queens, seeing them more as "sexual radicals" than as depressing losers. (Warhol, *POPism*)

> Why aren't they attacking dancers and fashion designers and interior decorators? Why us? when all I have to do is turn on my TV to see hundreds of actors who are so gay you can't believe your eyes and nobody bothers *them*. [...] Naturally, the Factory had fags; we were in the entertainment business and—That's Entertainment! (Warhol, *POPism*)

The attitude of Pop art in the '60s is typified as passive, making oneself translucent to the environment. But passivity, as a means of control through submission, implies that a pose must be taken on, an active position of being passive. In Warhol's silkscreens of Marilyn, Liz Taylor, Mick Jagger, etc., the cut-outs of color superimposed over the photographic image give the impression of a suppression of depth.

The real photo image can be seen underneath the overlaid, designed areas of color. "Apart from everything else, with her hair unnaturally fitted like a wig Marilyn looks like a transvestite" (Peter Gidal). Warhol is not merely giving a "representation of a representation of reality" (showing the lack of distinction between reality and the artificial), he is also entertaining us. Warhol, who began as a commercial artist, was always, and still is, a part of the conjurors of the consumer market. The Abstract Expressionists of the '50s followed the tradition of toughness. "It went with [...] fist fights about their work and their love lives" (Warhol). As they became successful, they moved out to the country to become closer to themselves and to their art. The scale of the work introduced a sense of private

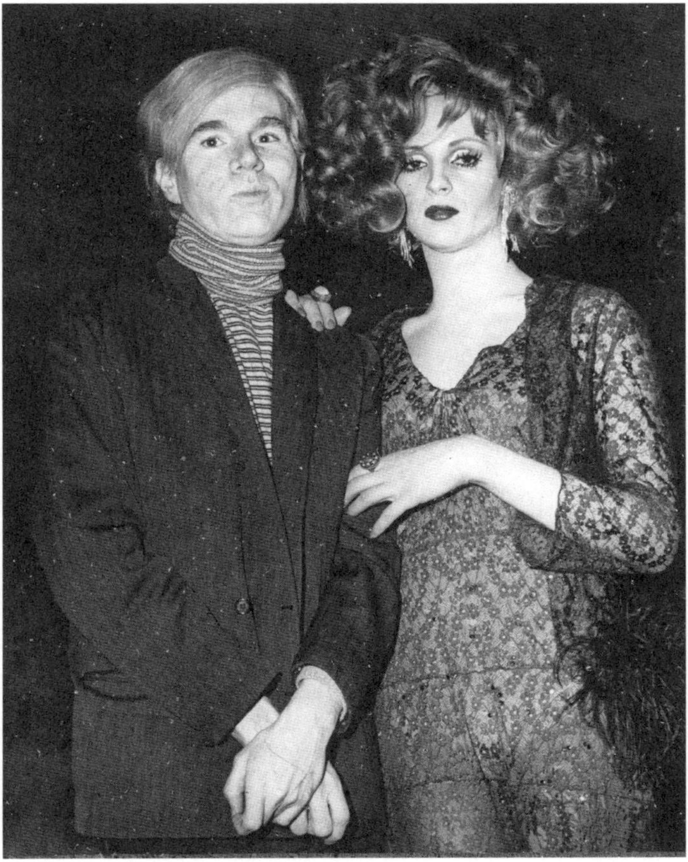

Andy Warhol and Candy Darling, 1969

spectacle to what was previously subjective investigation, making the work marketable alongside advertising and cinema.

The identity searching in the '60s that helped bring about women's liberation in the '70s encouraged the American woman/housewife to have an independent sex life. The media helped a great deal—a new kind of sanitary protection was discovered and packaged with her in mind. All kinds of "new" sexual fantasies were created for this "new" woman. Writers, like Erica Jong, wrote trashy novels for the sophisticated woman (supposedly *all* women), but her leading character was upper middle class—a writer. Women's desires were unleashed, creating a new merchandising angle for all sorts of commodities from floor wax and fashion to art.

The majority of new galleries are run by women. The majority of art buyers and private dealers are women. The majority of successful, new artists are young men. These artists, who, in art school and early careers concentrated on performance, installations, films, and other, more investigative activities, are now drawing and painting. They have accepted the demands of the art market for paintings—the art form of the bourgeoisie. Not since World War II and the end of fascism has there been such a demand for painting. During the war, women were forced to take over jobs that were previously the province of men. The Abstract Expressionists "created" subjectivity and monumental scale; but their overt machismo revealed their insecurities as men. "The art world sure was different in those days. I tried to imagine myself in a bar striding over to, say, Roy Lichtenstein and asking him to 'step outside' because I'd heard he'd insulted my soup cans" (Warhol).

Warhol was a chameleon in his passivity, willing to accept any persona given him. He hung around stars, so he *became* a star. On the other hand, David Bowie was actively changing his "star" persona. Where Warhol wanted anonymity as his personality, Bowie shed his past, remaking himself into something that would appeal to both sexes. Dressing as a woman, he appealed to heterosexual men who could get off on fantasizing about homosexual relations, enjoying the spectacle of Bowie, desiring him as man/woman for the duration of the performance. Women could get excited because he displayed himself as a daring man; to take on the qualities of femininity and yet still project such power as a performer meant a certain masculine setting—the excitement of a voyeur, witnessing somebody's subjectivity manifesting itself as drag. Though he was not the first rock performer to do this, he was the first to do it with conviction, making sexual exploration personal, and therefore palatable to a wide audience. Even dressed like a man, his streamlined appearance always suggested an unreality within his guise. As the character he portrays in *The Man Who Fell to Earth*, to be a human to him means unreality; his androgyny is very innocent. Candy Clark, wholesome America, begins by mothering him; later the relationship becomes distorted and sadomasochistic, very extreme and surreal. Bowie's sexual identity of androgyny, equated with sci-fi in the film, adds to his stage persona as the "new" man. Bowie *becomes* the future in the '70s.

The queens of the '60s dressed as their image of old Hollywood starlets. Bowie updated the look, making it futuristic. It was utopian and it was the Hollywood that never existed ... glitter rock. He took from Warhol, his subjectivity (objectivity?) and projected a super-subjectivity that he wore like an emblem, changing costumes (like a woman) to enhance his "moods." David Bowie is the double image of a Warhol painting.

III

After the happenings which began in the '60s, performance art took hold in the '70s. Vito Acconci was one of the first artists influenced by rock who incorporated it directly into his work; the first artist to overtly exploit sex the way, say, Jim Morrison or Iggy Pop did—employing shock tactics to gain control of the audience. More especially, his subversive, masochistic position forced the audience, as voyeurs, to become the controllers and receivers of guilt, making himself the hero (Christ-figure). In his *Conversions* work screened at CalArts, the hair is burned off his breasts: "A girl kneels behind me; I acquire a female form by inserting, losing, my penis in her mouth: exercising my body in its new stance (social activities change by means of another persona: change by means of the kind of person I am attempting to change into)." Here, there are two not necessarily opposing situations created. The first is the masochistic one, like the '60s suicidal rock stars who abused their bodies with drugs and alcohol to work themselves into the right state of communion with their audience. What could be more painful than giving up one's identity? Secondly, "every transvestite feels superior because, underneath, they know that they are men" (Rechy). These attitudes were alienating to women in the art world, but his influence on the male students—an attitude of reigning masculinity—was subconscious.

The subject matter of Michael Glier, Robert Longo, and Jeff Wall is masculinity—both its subversion and its reconventionalization as fashion/commodity.

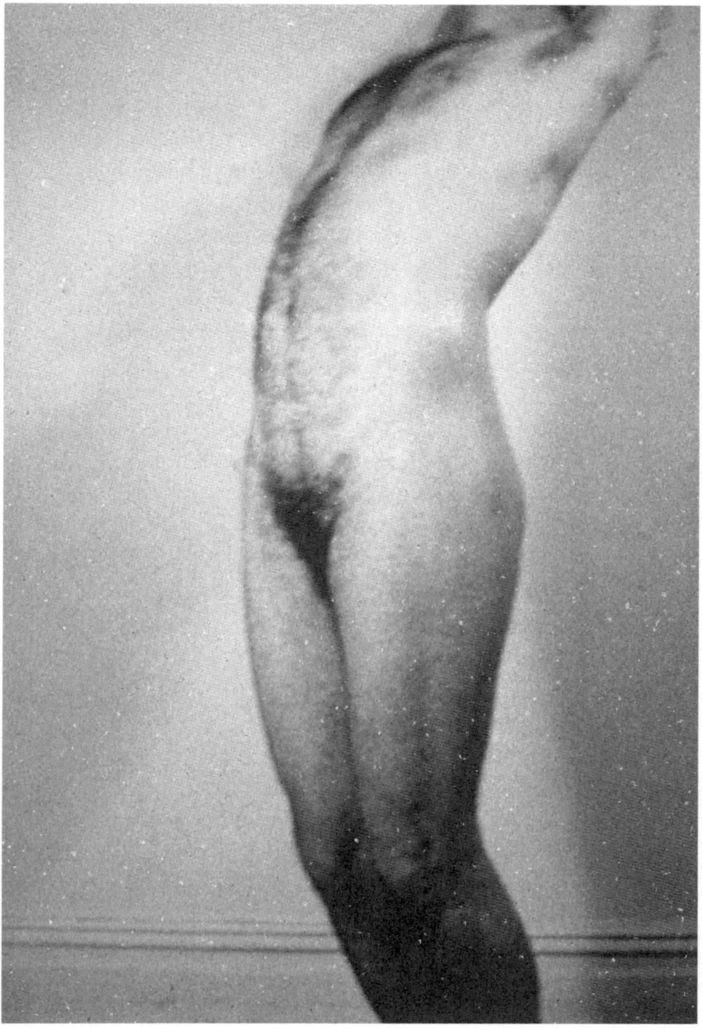

Vito Acconci, still from *Conversions*, 1971

Eric Bogosian, a New York performance artist, slides back and forth between homosexual "macho" and the "new" man. In his sequence of vignettes, there is a sequence between an Iggy Pop contest where he and Joe Hannan dance around on stage, holding sticks like guitars and baseball bats, to male-strip-act-type music. Eric comes out on stage wearing a boxer's robe. It is not clear whether it is for a male disco or for the women in the audience. He winks and smiles and eventually the women give him catcalls.

Michael Glier's first works—large chalk drawings—seemed to be crusading against the evil of white male power and appealing to the liberals' guilt complexes. His forceful, aggressive, expressionistic strokes could be paralleled to Bogosian's ironic, new, macho homosexual who parodies the straight world. The pictures show the old stereotypes of the heterosexual macho man. The attitude in the work is similar to Acconci's identity reversal, taking on the woman's viewpoint to eliminate guilt (but, like the transvestite, knowing he is really male makes him feel superior). Also, like the transvestite who is concerned with his/her own identity more than any sexual activity, Glier is, in the process, making himself into a hero for the feminists by parodying old macho stereotypes. At the same time, he takes up the position of the new macho man.

On the cover of David Bowie's record *Heroes*, he portrays a hero figure/rock star striking a pose, with one hand drawn narcissistically to his chest and the other raised in a salute to imagined fans/followers of his make-believe religion. His head is tilted down and the eyes are keenly focused, commanding the power of a Hitler. His skin is an unnatural white, contrasted against the black leather jacket. Like all expressionistic work, there is an ambiguity of orientation in Glier's work.

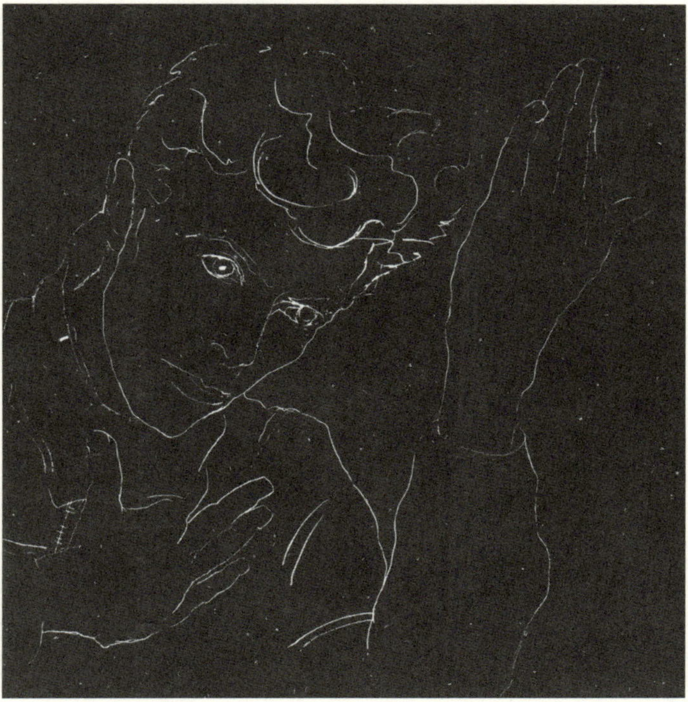

Kim Gordon, *Heroes*, ca. 1983

He seems unaware of his position in relation to the system. He is set apart from other men by taking on attitudes formerly attributed to women artists, yet he is set apart from women because he is a man, in a heroic position. In creating this distance, a situation occurs for desire towards him/his paintings for women/male collectors/buyers.

A question at this point might be, what makes art with subject matter about masculinity and its varying shades of playful femininity saleable? And why can this art only be done by men? One answer lies in the belief/(conditioned) system towards female sexuality. Women's sexuality is only conceptual, whereas men's is real. People want to buy something real. There continues to be support for women artists who show in galleries whose pictures are conceptually related—but mostly the support comes from the academic sphere of the art world.

Robert Longo's work is sometimes about male bonding and perhaps manifests a desire to express and elevate masculinity in much the same way that some feminists bond together to elevate femaleness. In his drawing series *Men in the Cities* (1979), the figures are caught in motion, tortured looking, suppressed in some kind of dance. Seen in a gallery, the pictures (often butted up against each other) appear as frozen film frames. The arms and legs angle out towards and past the edges. It is unclear whether they are retracting from or progressing towards some unseen thing or person. The men wear black suits and ties, the asexual sign of masculinity. The women (drawn in a very masculine manner) wear dresses and fit in naturally as fashion plates; they are simply the token other half of the men. Although the suits symbolize anonymity, the men pictured are clearly all young men and their hair and movements coincide with the style that evolved out of

’50s rock ’n’ roll and the subsequent street culture—tight pants, leather jackets, and hair extended to a curl at the top of the head. This was one of the first new, overt signs of male sexuality in modern society.

The notion of women as fashion is an abstraction. Previously in film, style change had been concentrated on women. But with David Bowie, the notion of men’s sexuality, now a part of fashion, attains the same level of abstraction. Male bonding out in the streets tends to wipe out any basis for sexual interaction—no gap, no barrier, no mystery, and so no sexual interest. Film sets up a distance that can allow eroticization to take place. As if Longo’s drawn figures are aware of this, they appear self-conscious. The drawing of two retro-looking rockers strangling each other, and the record cover for Glenn Branca’s *The Ascension*, are the “closest you can get to two men fucking.” In film as in art, physical contact between men is only acceptable if it is violent. Longo seems to be coding this gesture of the two men fighting/fucking, subverting the illusion of conventional heterosexual masculinity, which is now placed in the realm of abstraction.

If this form of masculinity (the ’50s style of man) displays certain aspects formerly valued as feminine (narcissism), it might follow that men could seek from other men an enjoyment of their equal sexuality. Bowie foregrounds an underlying and typically adolescent message of rock ’n’ roll: that if the world is ending, any form of behavior is permissible. This makes possible a free enjoyment by men of their sexual potentials. On the one hand, Longo, through allusion to the freed, male sexuality of rock ’n’ roll, suggests these radical possibilities; on the other, he is restricted from deeper exploration by the position of art as a part of the adult, real world.

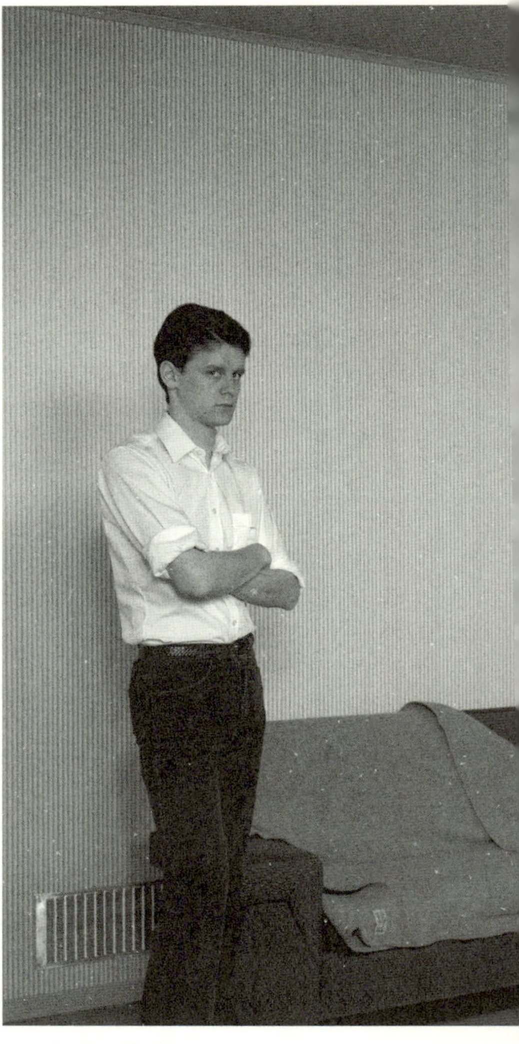

Jeff Wall, *Double Self-Portrait*, 1979

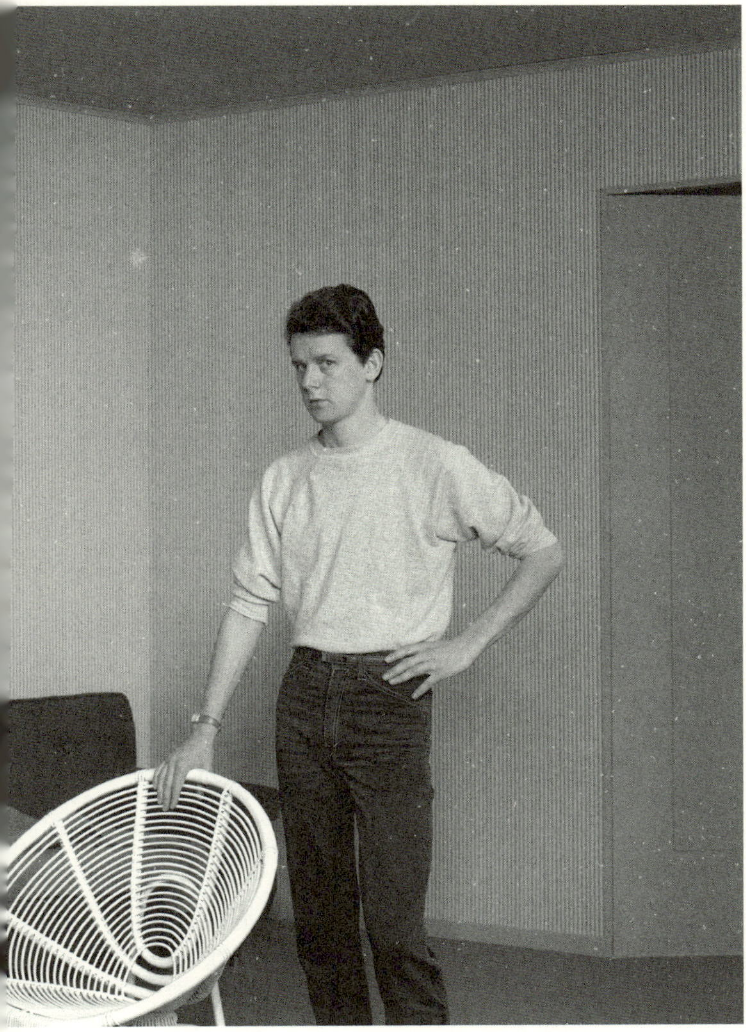

Jeff Wall, a slightly older artist, takes the viewpoint of the homosexual in art, relating it to the role of the homosexual as commercial contriver within the commodity system. "The homosexual contriver stands in a powerful, if fictitious position in speaking to each sex from the standpoint of the other. He is displaced from sexual systems and, within his particular sphere, seems to subject it to his discourse which is inherently inverted, or mirrored an opposite" (Wall, *Problems*). The homosexual middle class of artists, writers, and stage designers—and their acceptance by the bourgeoisie of the nineteenth century with its development (the decorative arts in particular) into the fashion industry—was based precisely on the notion that they directed their art towards the leisure class to the heterosexual, upper-class women. By directing it at the women, it also included the man/husband. "Fashion couture [...] is the cultural activity which constitutes the being of bourgeois woman; it is the industry of construction of being woman (of course this being is being for man)." Wall is saying that the outsider (homosexual) is using the artifice of woman, transforming himself into a situation for dialogue with the heterosexual male. Remaining a man, as well, he speaks man to man, the image of woman being an extension of his illusory position. The product, woman, projected from him, has a separate identity or is his mirrored "fictitious" identity. In his work *Double Self-Portrait* (1979), Wall appears twice within the image. Like all his work it is a giant, Cibachrome transparency, backlit with fluorescent lighting and secured in a case/frame.

The transparency comprises two halves joined in the middle. On the viewer's right side, he stands closer in the foreground, one hand held on his hip, the other hand rests on a circular hypnotic chair. The white cane chair is placed off-center but its vortex lines up with the corner of the room/stage set. On the other side, he stands further back, arms crossed, wearing a pristine white shirt. Because he is out of center focus, he appears to be presenting the situation as auteur, but his shirt clearly matches the chair, making him part of the seduction of the presentation. By switching clothes he is inverting the roles of model and producer, creating an unsettling atmosphere. Who is the chair for? Is it for a woman about to meet her maker and/or master? Or is it for a man being beckoned out of the sphere of the home into the public spectacle to meet his unseen conspirators? Wall's streamlined Bowie-like appearance adds to the confusion between his own public projection of homosexuality against his private heterosexual life, creating a seductive ambiguity.

As much as Jeff Wall is exposing the source of heterosexual sensibility as gay through this presentation, he is also recreating a further desirability for women, previously found in fashion, emanating from out of rock 'n' roll. The woman becomes a voyeur and can identify with the man (Wall) in the same way she identifies with female fashion models and mannequins, imaging herself in the same exhibitionist, public situation that holds the illusion of power.

> The decorative arts, by historical definition new, directed primarily at the upper-middle-class home and therefore at the wife (the constructed male woman), that is, at the private sphere, protected by the rights of the (private) citizen in liberal constitutional ideology, could "freely" elaborate such themes (the investigation of the structure of the modern self). But their freedom was constrained, defined and organized, not by state ("public") regulation, but by the

> fashionable market itself: that is, by the ebb and flow of the social (and political) struggle within the bourgeois couple, which is the engine of fashion. (Wall, *Problems*)

Wall, whose work is too large and too expensive to maintain, belongs to the realm of the home, but realistically can only exist in the public ("state") domain. Like a store window display, its items suggesting attainable utopias when purchased for the home, the work's unattainability suggests an impossibility, creating instead a monument/sign for the unresolved desire.

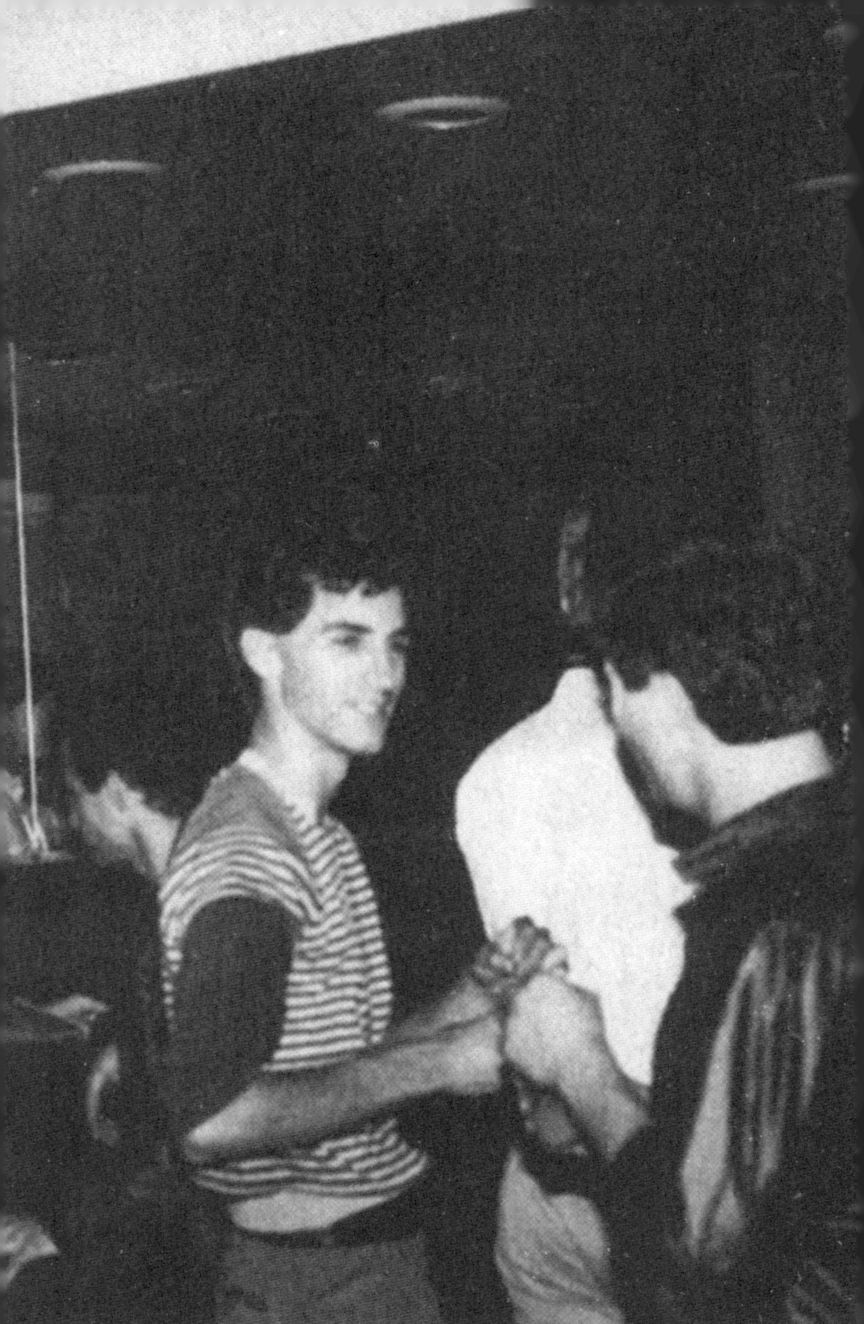

Making the Nature Scene: Rock Clubs in New York

Andy Warhol produced the Velvet Underground's first record and shows. In an atmosphere of "happenings" and multimedia events, he created the first chic rock-club environments, mixing art with music, uptown with downtown. "So now [...] we were reaching people in all parts of town, all different types of people: the ones who saw the movies would get curious about the gallery show, and the kids dancing at the Dom would want to see the movies. [...] It was fun to see the Museum of Modern Art people next to the teeny-boppers next to the amphetamine queens next to the fashion editors" (Andy Warhol, *POPism*, 1980).

The effect of Warhol's idea of repackaging art as interior design and decoration can be seen as clubs become the new alternative spaces. In the history of architecture the skyscraper, besides being efficient in the use of space, encapsulated the notion of having within its many floors a wide array of functions: it was a self-sufficient entity. Today the rock club makes use of its many levels: each floor has a different function, each can be used to evoke a different time period. By continually renovating, opening up new floors and redecorating old ones, each club vies for the position of the most favored venue. Rock clubs have become an alternative to the "alternative spaces" of the art world.

As New York rock clubs become the new alternative spaces, video monitors become standard design accessories. Many

Originally published in *Artists' Architecture: Scenes and Conventions* (London: Institute of Contemporary Arts, 1983). A similar text appears in Gordon's video, *Making the Nature Scene* (shot and edited by Tony Oursler, 1983).

Left: Danceteria, New York, date unknown

believe that clubs are as important as museums and alternative spaces as an outlet for artists' videos, even if the work is taken in a looser vein. The videos are used to prevent the customers from leaving, to entertain them while they are waiting for the "main attraction." The lounge atmosphere is used in an attempt to make them feel that they are at home, or in somebody else's luxurious home where they would feel comfortably extravagant.

Video employed on a monumental scale elevates the image and its technology to the subordination of all else. Two years ago PiL (Public Image Ltd) performed at the Ritz rock club where they used the giant video screen both as a barrier between them and the audience and also as the central focus of the performance. They alternated live shots of themselves taken from behind the screen with prerecorded video images. The audience, not willing to accept this representation of a performance, destroyed the screen.

These clubs provide an outlet for video art because there is no comparable outlet in the art world itself. For artists, showing videos or performing in clubs seems to offer the possibility of affecting a part of the "real world." But because of the utopian nature of the club environment, it is difficult for the work to be taken seriously. Instead of affecting the "real world," it remains trapped within the bounds of a playground environment. Clubs, like alternative spaces, gain institutional power through what they promote or sponsor. In the end, "alternative spaces" such as The Kitchen or Fashion Moda become better known than anything they show, and in a similar way rock clubs gain prestige through their art events. The clubs attract a non-art-world audience who do not know why it is "chic" to be there, but just that they *should* be there.

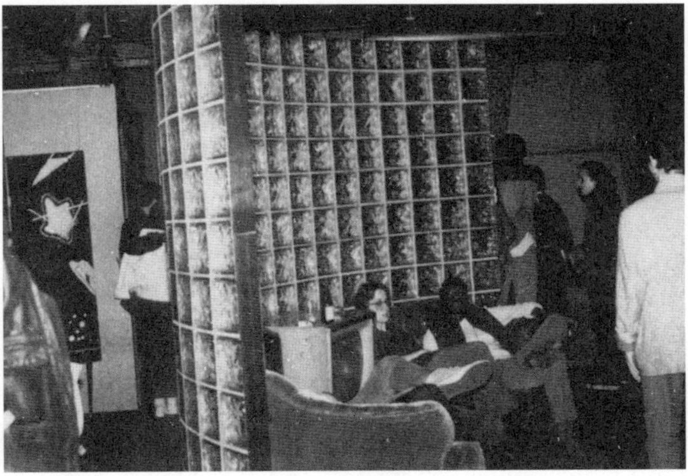

Danceteria, New York, date unknown

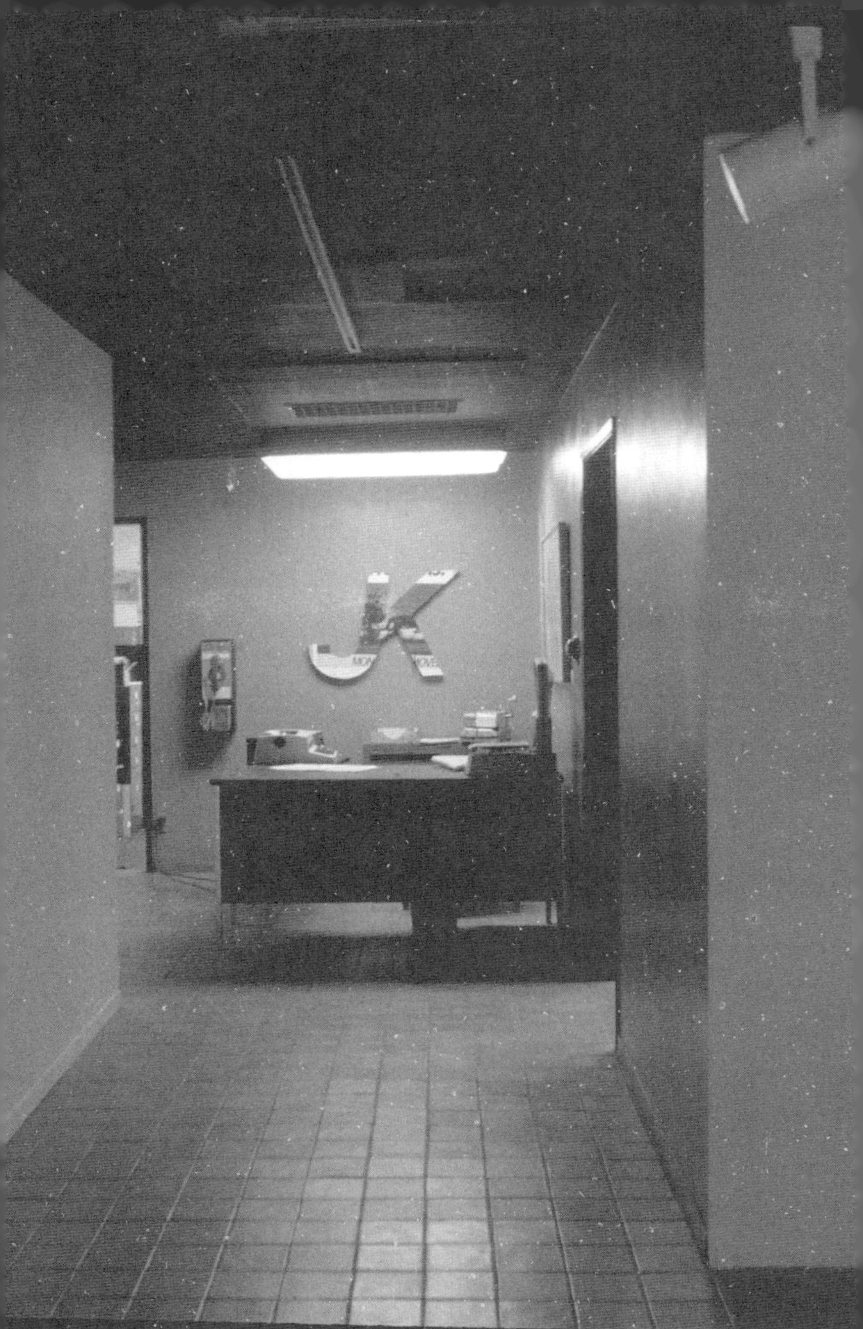

Turning the Conversation

> Rationalism is necessary like order, but whatever the order, it can be upset by the external factors of another order—whether historical, geological, psychological.
> —Aldo Rossi

In Los Angeles an illusion of rationality or order has evolved through the use of designed displays in an otherwise boundaryless desertscape. To live in this kind of environment, which borders on the sci-fi, where design has impregnated your private memories and images, where the visual exterior doesn't stop at your front door, is to become slightly irrational or schizophrenic. Because of the vastness of Los Angeles things are seen only in fragments, without a sense of the whole except through the repetition of advertising logos and billboard images. The designed display sensibility embodies the utopia that is not possible, finalizing the irrationality of the individual. It is easy to see how someone here becomes obsessed with the redirection of design. John Knight is one of these artists. As in the work of Ed Ruscha, the art takes its content from its environment, Los Angeles, rather than any one art formalism. To be influenced by the surroundings and then to let these obsessions, perversions, and passions in turn affect the work, leads to art that is less pure but is perhaps more interesting, as it opens up the possibility for other thoughts. Although LA is

Originally published in *Journal: A Contemporary Art Magazine* 4, no. 40 (Fall 1984). The essay appeared within a section of the magazine that functioned as the catalogue for John Knight's exhibition at the Los Angeles Institute of Contemporary Art (LAICA), the independent art space that produced *Journal*. The cover of the magazine was designed by Knight as part of the exhibition.

Left: John Knight, *Project for Los Angeles Institute of Contemporary Art*, 1984, installation view

similar in many ways to any large suburban city, it is unique in both its perversion of the *new* and its inability to really escape from the past. Even though the media alludes to a sense of freedom, the psychological makeup is one of Midwest repression. The copy (advertising) exists with the original conception (the American dream) as a sign exclaiming both individual freedom and an announcement of its death. Even as the object or image arouses memories that lead to other events and other lives, this speaks of the past and not the city of the future. There is no dialectic between the old and the new, no difference between the representation and the re-representation. Instead, the two combine and evolve into a "do it yourself" sensibility, which is the lifestyle of a pioneer, symbolic of a retreat or link with the past. The result is an abundance of customization, and the stylized aesthetic of the tract communities that take on various generic design traits relating them geographically to the small towns across the country from which most everyone has come.

John Knight's work for his exhibition at LAICA is an embellishment of the alternative space. By displaying LAICA's many contradictions and the complexity of its situation in purpose and direction, an analogy is made to the city itself. Like many alternative spaces, LAICA is a sort of "do it yourself" business that has to appeal to both the community and the corporate business world as a viable and fundable organization. Conventionally it is the gallery that designs the scenario within which the artist places his/her work. If the exhibition is a good one, then the space is a good one. In Knight's redesign of the space he is exaggerating what is inherent within the ideological and psychological makeup of LAICA, making it into a set for whatever may unfold.

As you enter the reception area, covering the wall opposite the door is a mural: a western frontier landscape. Superimposed on the mural is "LAICA" and underneath the tagline, "When the Conversation Turns to Art." The western pioneer imagery was chosen as a symbolic shared spirit between LAICA and corporate advertising aesthetics, such as those of Marlboro, Western Federal Savings, and Wells Fargo. For the corporation, it functions by presenting a cohesiveness, as in the Wells Fargo ad wherein the image shows the original Wells Fargo stagecoach bringing information and paychecks from the East to the West and stopping at isolated outposts of civilization along the way. It presents the corporation as a primary force in making possible what now exits. Superimposed on this scenario of the past is the photo advertising technology of the present. This strategy of the image appears on corporate billboards throughout the city and extends the locus of the corporation, becoming a part of the exterior architecture of the city. Through their repetition they create the sense of momentum and the illusion of a series of events: heroic service. For LAICA the isolated display of the mural represents a fragment of its concerns: corporate visibility and the evolution or progress of the alternative space toward a state of higher visibility within the community and on an international level. Because LAICA is not a corporation nor a commercial venture on any level, not even big enough to qualify as a museum, it remains as a makeshift *business-oriented* concern. Within the existing elements of the reception area, such as the carpeted walls, monumentalized reception desk, and the sliding glass doors that open onto a homey patio, where flowers and plants are somewhat overgrown, can be seen the contradictions between an attempt at corporate office style and California home living. It is these conflicting values that Knight has embellished as an artist taking on the role of the designer. After all, "Ask not what your country can do for you, but what you can do for your country."

As in all of John Knight's work, detail is very important. Detail gives realism to otherwise fictional, theoretical, and, therefore, abstract ideas. The framed presentation of LAICA's letterhead/stationary is part of the mood, as is the use of the small adjoining gallery. A small business might display its letterhead; a corporation wouldn't. However, a corporation would have a room to display their current projects and past accomplishments. LAICA's display/entrance gallery remains empty, the memory of a corporate display experience. As the redesign centers around the reception area, it returns the space back metaphorically to its original residential structure.

In its present evolution LAICA can be seen as analogous to a villa structure … complete with corridors and a rambling ambiance that suggests a multitude of mysterious events and an eliteness of class that doesn't correspond to LAICA's plea for public interaction and monetary dependence. As an archetypal house structure, LAICA is reduced to the one-event idea that a house traditionally holds. As Knight proposes, that one event is the exteriorization of LAICA, changed to serve as a placement/service concern. This reflects LAICA's desired interaction with the community, analogous to the way media images are internalized within one's private thoughts and refracted in one's home design. The mural image begins to take on its own meaning for LAICA (the shed structure in the picture now symbolizes the original house … LAICA's ancestry) as the space is redesigned to correspond to the images within interior decorating and architecture magazines, which represent some ideal utopia. The interiors in the magazines are often designed for the finality of the magazine displays. Knight's

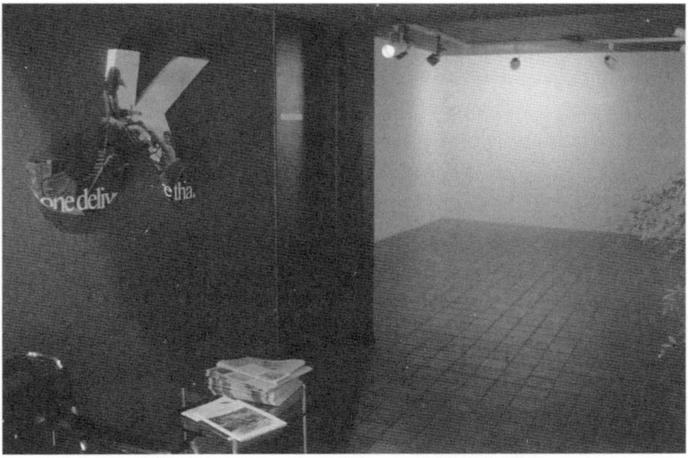

John Knight, *Project for Los Angeles Institute of Contemporary Art*, 1984, installation view

use of the rectangular perspective of the reception area, with the desk framing the mural, is a three-dimensional experience of a magazine. It is this area where the subjective element within advertising media is confused with the individual's experience of the subjective, where the work becomes most like science fiction in which all the preoccupation with detail marks the realism of today.

Three conventional wall reliefs of Knight's, used in other shows, repeat themselves here, but the surface motif has been changed to reflect the present content: LAICA. Previously done for Documenta 7, the wood reliefs cut in the shape of his initials JK were then wrapped with glossy travel posters advertising different countries. "The posters glued to the wood surface covered the 'JK' monogram almost completely but where the rectangular paper came to an end at the tips of the 'J' or the 'K' the deliberately hand-crafted 'original' quality of the underlying work was revealed. [...] By placing them on the walls of the successive staircase landings of the Museum Fridericianum building, Knight treated the eight sets of initials, intended as a single work, like signs."[1] Now the 'JK's are wrapped with the western landscape images. The first relief the viewer sees hangs in LAICA's reception area. In the context of LAICA and this exhibition, it is "high" art but is also reminiscent of reception-area decor being set against the carpeted wall covering. Another relief is placed just outside the public area but within view at the end of the hall that leads to the inner offices. Along these walls, not visible to the public, with the exception of one corner wall, is a collection of various artists' works donated to LAICA. Collectively they are referred to as "The

1 Anne Rorimer, *John Knight* (Chicago: Renaissance Society of the University of Chicago, 1983), n.p.

Building Fund" (the sale of the work produces funds for the maintenance of the alternative space). This relief marks LAICA's past. The third relief has been placed in a Wells Fargo bank branch in Santa Monica in a small seating alcove where art is normally hung on the wall. The use of the latter space is one of the primary interests that have been voiced by the director of the institute to be pursued as future concerns.

Like the work of architect Aldo Rossi, Knight is concerned with the topography of the object. One cannot describe an artwork without describing all events surrounding it. To describe the topography of Los Angeles is to describe its media. The dynamics of the topography are expressed here through the changes in scale. From the wall mural to the desk to the stationary to the wall reliefs and finally to the cover of the catalogue ... the image changes from the monumental to the personal ... from the interior (strategy) to the exterior (relief) ... from the public (LAICA catalogue) to the privacy of the home ... from the real past to the filmic (mural) to the facade of the interior of LAICA. As its front and back cover, the frontier-pioneer imagery wrapping the catalogue/*Journal* issue blends in on the newsstands with other nonprofessional-type publications like *Arizona Highways* or *Southern California Living*, and LAICA achieves, finally, a credible corporate image outside itself. Placed within the designated section for art magazines whose covers display art as design, the *Journal* cover stands apart, looking misplaced. In this generic setting it is the content, finally, that determines its usefulness or merit ... from individual to individual, it becomes aligned with other orders.

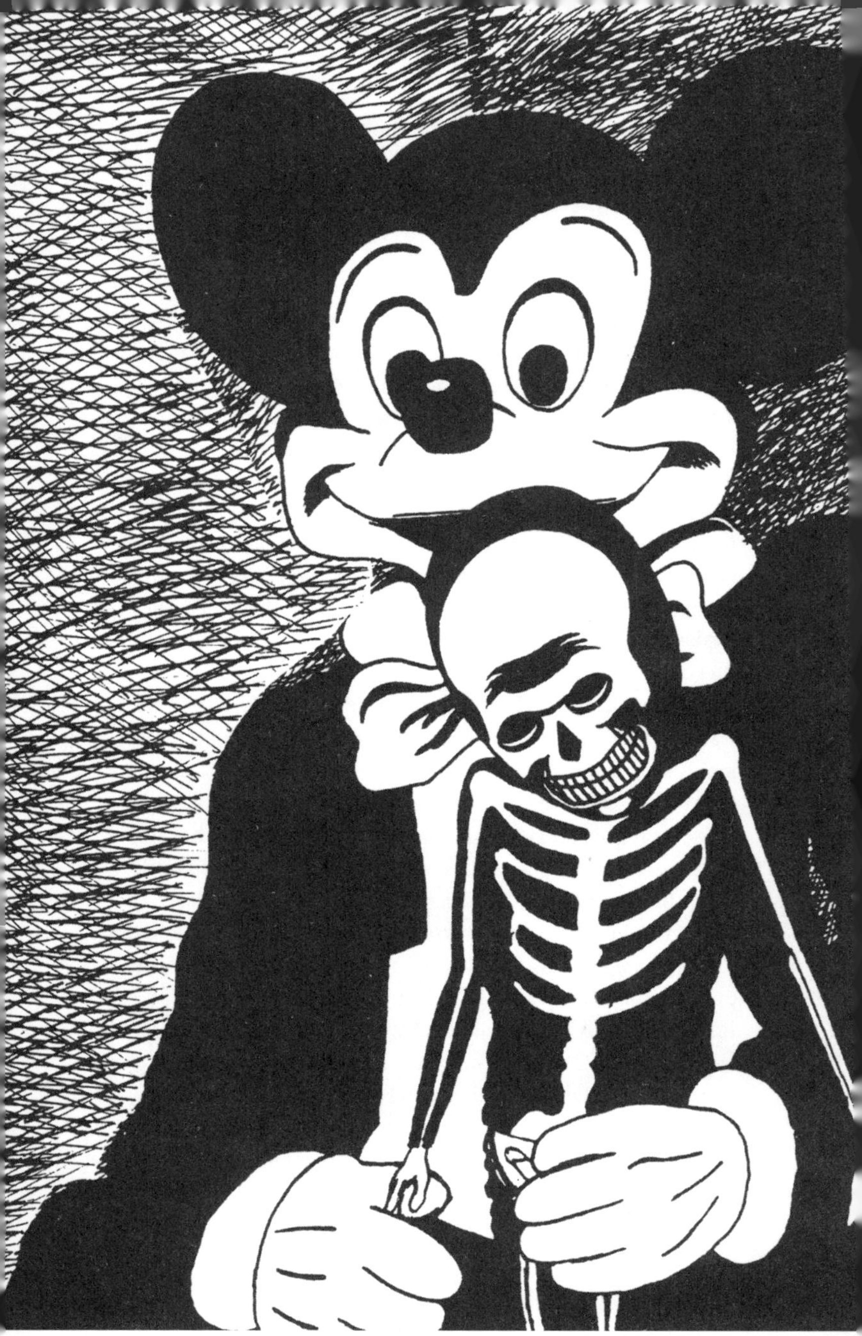

American Prayers

Mickey Mouse, Marilyn Monroe, and Coca-Cola T-shirts are still popular all over the world, proving America's ability to sell an image. But in the '60s the youth of America, disillusioned with the American way, sought to escape from all this by returning to past ideas of communal living and to slogans of love and peace. Incredible violence surrounded the times. Aside from the Vietnam War there were the Kennedy and King assassinations, and a steady stream of violent protest demonstrations. On the level of popular culture there were such events as the mysterious death of Brian Jones and the Rolling Stones' tour that culminated with the deaths at Altamont. And then there was Charles Manson and "the Family." Many people who didn't die in the upheavals of those years remain as casualties of the '60s, maimed either by drugs or the Vietnam War. During this time Pop art perpetuated the myth of America as an eternally "new" culture. Its representation of America as an entity of the moment perpetuated a pseudostate of no-history, and the American dream of innocence. In retrospect most Pop art appears to have reinforced the status quo, because it ceased to examine the America beneath the icons it adopted.

Although in the beginning Pop art's ironic strategy was to glorify the image of America's surface, its larger-than-life exaggerations brought out the violence of consumerism. But the shock value and absurdity of these images made the cultural critique ambiguous and entertaining. It was the music of the '60s that really hinted at what lurked beneath the American dream. Within the seeming wholesomeness of surf music and

Originally published in *Artforum* 23, no. 8 (April 1985). © Artforum.

Left: Raymond Pettibon, untitled drawing from *Virgin Fears*, 1983

the Beach Boys' brand of happy, suburban-kids' music there was "Cease to Exist," the song Manson wrote. In Neil Young's songs, the music seduced with the illusion of a drug-induced happy state of nature. But the lyrics—of "The Old Laughing Lady," for example—expressed an unease within this borrowed utopian system of escape:

> There's a fever on the freeway, blacks out the night.
> There's a slipping on the stairway just don't feel right.
> And there's a rumbling in the bedroom and a flashing
> of the light.
> There's the old laughing lady everything is alright.[1]

"The old laughing lady" is a symbol for drugs.

The migration west to the land of psychedelia triggered the music that expressed the contradictions of those times. The San Francisco, Haight-Ashbury scene of drugs, love, and peace quickly turned sour. Manson, among the quickest to surmise the end, fled south to Los Angeles, heading for Paradise—suburbia. LA's lush landscaping only begins to make sense when you realize that underneath it is a desert. LA is Ed Ruscha's desert on fire. His paintings are analogous to that era of apocalyptic music: Bob Dylan's "Desolation Row," the Doors' "The End," and the drug death of Gram Parsons culminating with his body being stolen and burned in the desert. And then, of course, there was Manson's use of the Beatles' "Helter Skelter." Manson and the Family were tried and convicted. The Vietnam War ended. Everything returned to "normal." By the '70s Jimi Hendrix and Janis Joplin were dead; Jim Morrison's death

1 From Neil Young, "The Old Laughing Lady," *Neil Young*, © 1969 Broken Arrow Music Corp. All song lyrics appear as they were originally printed in *Artforum*.

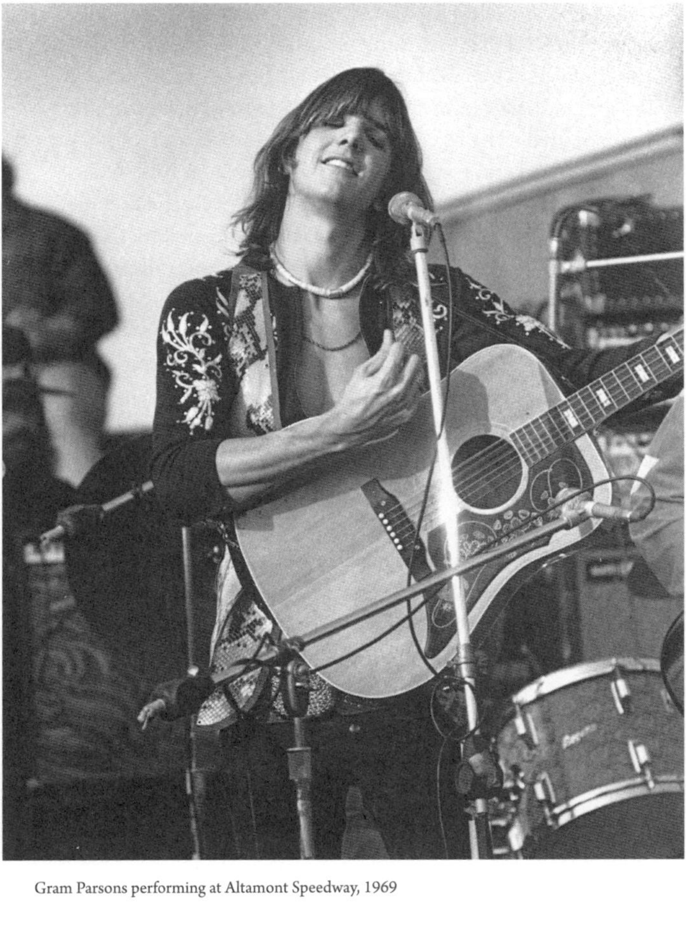

Gram Parsons performing at Altamont Speedway, 1969

followed. Corporate rock began to grow. It wasn't until the end of the '70s that the "punk movement" was fabricated by England's Malcolm McLaren, who made it fashion. McLaren took what he saw in a few American groups—the Ramones, Richard Hell and the Voidoids, and the New York Dolls—and packaged it in the form of the Sex Pistols, whose music proclaimed anarchy and the end of rock 'n' roll. The first real punk or anarchy group actually was the Stooges, which came out of Detroit's high-energy garage-music scene at the end of the '60s. Among their contemporaries were the MC5 and Alice Cooper. When the Stooges' first record came out in 1969 they were considered submoronic, and stood out from everything else. By the beginning of the '80s, local groups in Los Angeles were beginning to mutate the form that had come to be known as British punk. Because LA has always been very conservative, there was never any reason to stop rebelling. In LA, weirdly dressed kids are seen as a threat to suburban, family life, while in England fashion is an escape from the distinctions of class. Each person's facade unites him or her with a certain music faction, each at odds with all others. In LA, even though there are different cliques—sometimes based simply on which suburbs the groups come from—they all are jumbled together as "the enemy," apart from the adult world. Just as in the '60s hippie decor was an affront to most people's sensibilities, now any derivation of it is looked upon with skepticism and as a reminder of the dissension of that era.

There is now a conspicuously growing nostalgia for the music of the '60s. Within the resurgence of music forms of that period (including surf, psychedelic, and heavy-metal acid guitar music), there is a message in the lyrics, which again reflect something other than that all is well in paradise. It seems every month there's a new derivation of the Velvet Underground coming out with a record from LA. The Cramps (originally from New York), who were also a big influence in LA, seem to have spawned a whole series of "Horror Rock" bands such as T.S.O.L., 45 Grave, Christian Death, and the Gun Club, with its references back to blues and the devil. The music of the Adolescents, a group from Orange County, combines the surf and psychedelic guitar music in a powerful sound which often achieves the uplifting feeling of the Byrds' music. The lyrics, though, are more direct in their disenchantment with commercial entertainment and the constructed popular culture of LA. For example, "L.A. Girl":

> We don't really care if you say we're too young
> We don't waste our time tanning in the sun
> We don't even care what you know or think
> Spoiled rich brat you ain't so neat
>
> *Chorus:*
> L.A. girl, L.A. world
> Don't tell us how to act
> Don't tell us what to wear
> L.A. girl, L.A. world
> You didn't create our scene.[2]

Or "Kids of the Black Hole":

> No sound is heard from unit two
> When there was once so much to do
> It was once a green mansion, but now it's a wasteland
> Our days of wreckless fun are through

2 From the Adolescents, "L.A. Girl," *The Adolescents,* © 1981 American Lesion Music.

Kids in a fast lane living for today
No rules to abide by and no rules to obey
Sex, drugs and fun is their only thought and care
Another swig of brew another overnight affair

Chorus:
House of the filthy
House not a home
House of destruction
Where the lurkers roamed
House that belonged
To all the homeless kids
Kids of the black hole

Messages and slogans are the primary decor
History's recorded in a clutter on the floor
Inhabitants that searched the grounds for roaches or spare
change
Another night of chaos is so easy to arrange

(Chorus)

The nights of birthdays
The nights of fry
The nights of endless drinking
The knights of violence
The knights of noise
The nights that had to end for good
Still not understood by the girls and boys

Carefree in their actions as for morals they had none
When the girls were horny who would be the lucky ones?

Pushing all the limits to a point of no return
Trashed beyond belief to show the kids don't wanna learn.[3]

Or Saccharine Trust's "We Don't Need Freedom":

we don't need freedom
we don't need freedom
we don't need freedom
freedom is what ruined your brain
with creativity drugs and pain
freedom is what let you run wild
explain freedom to your fatherless child
we don't need freedom
do we now

freedom preaches disobedience
idiot rebellion false allegiance
pride waste lust and greed
we're free to obey all of these
comfortably that's how we'll be
enough for you plenty for me
we don't need actors and rock stars
all we'll want is farmers and soldiers.[4]

These groups set up their own record labels and fanzines, and make their own music instead of waiting for the latest corporate A and R men to come to town and package them. They have very different attitudes from those of the rock 'n' roll groups of the '60s. For example, there is a faction of the hard-

3 From the Adolescents, "Kids of the Black Hole," *The Adolescents*, © 1981 American Lesion Music.

4 From Saccharine Trust, "We Don't Need Freedom," *Paganicons*, © 1981 SST Records.

core movement from Washington, DC, that is referred to as "straight edge." These kids are antidrugs, antidrinking, anti-Reagan, and antisex—not so much out of puritanism as from a desire to be in control, and to avoid being manipulated by the consumerist system. These groups represent America's tradition of horror, coming from Edgar Allan Poe and his anti-bourgeois, antifamily stories of incest. The groups that have most successfully taken from a wide range of American music—folk, jazz, blues, the sensuous anarchy of acid guitar—and who combine it all in a savagery of primal emotions to express modern apocalyptic doom are the Minutemen, Black Flag, Saccharine Trust, and the Meat Puppets. In his review of Black Flag's album *Damaged* (*The Village Voice*, December 30, 1981–January 5, 1982), Doug Simmons wrote, "It's difficult to sympathize with the rage of California's hardcore, a scene populated mostly by the sons of upper middle-class white sub-urbanites." Then, later: "More than any album, *Damaged* articulates and justifies hardcore, especially if you accept insanity as a defense." In the version of the song "Damaged" sung by Henry Rollins, Black Flag's present vocalist, he talks, over the intro, about his father, who he says used to drive him out to the country and make him recite the Pledge of Allegiance over and over.

Raymond Pettibon is a resident artist at SST Records, started by members of Black Flag. Besides producing record covers and posters for SST, New Alliance, and Thermidor (the three companies work together), he also published books of his drawings, which are available through SST's catalogue. Wandering outside the realm of the art world and attached to a music subculture, Pettibon can depict a wider range of subject matter than is considered appropriate or even possible within the avant-garde of the art world, because of the inhibiting val-

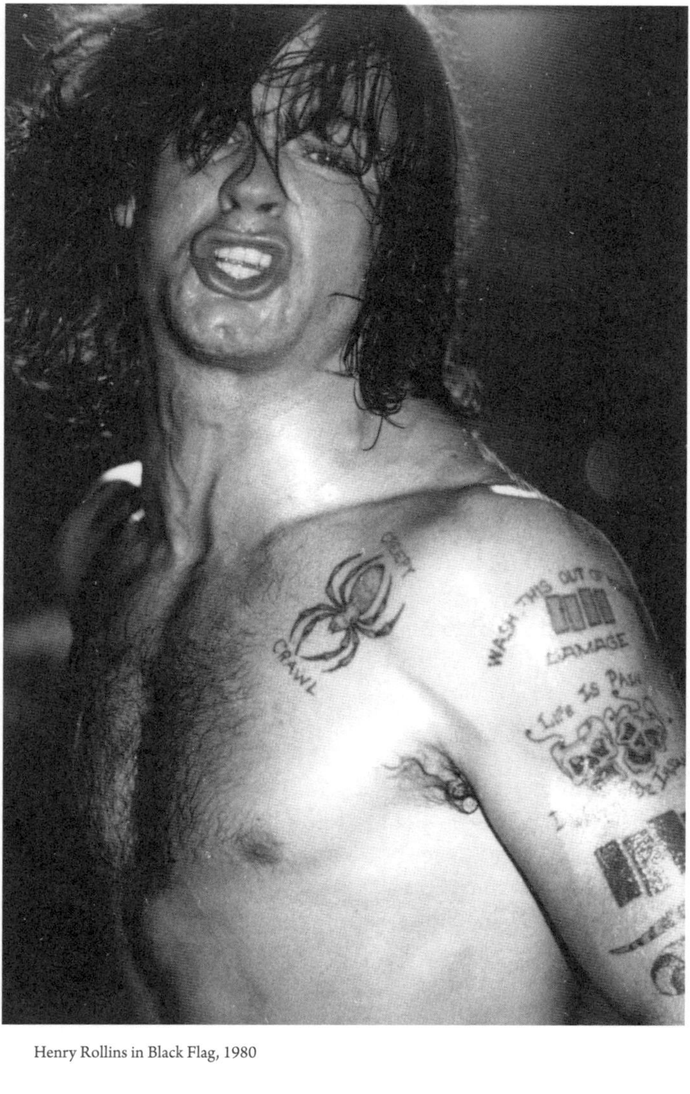

Henry Rollins in Black Flag, 1980

ues that prevail in that system. Pettibon's drawings all have texts of one-liner punch lines with a twist. The pictures are like stills edited out of a longer story. They can be seen specifically as comic strips based on the music of Black Flag and the Minutemen, but since they are not really done for the groups but are taken from Pettibon's vast collection, they are ultimately statements unto themselves. The drawings feed off the simplistic morals of made-for-TV movies, which center around "contemporary" questions. Pettibon doesn't feel that the themes of the drawings are his inventions. They are meant to be clichés, unconscious scenes or situations which have appeared before. A poster for Black Flag taken from one of Pettibon's drawings shows in the foreground an androgynous-looking person with an insane smile on her/his face. In the background is the unhappy face of a boy.

Pettibon was only twelve at the end of the '60s, but the events of that decade provide one of the prominent themes in his work. There are recurring Manson-like figures, with followers who wear the familiar *X* on their foreheads. Using illustration's technique of image snowballing, in which certain elements are repeated in different drawings, the meaning of the images builds and changes from picture to picture, setting up a language of its own. Pettibon's use of Manson to relate to the culture of the '80s is akin to the use, by the punk movement of the '70s, of bondage—not to advocate it but to show that they were in bondage by society. Now this LA subculture feels crossed out by the suburban, middle-class paradisiacal state of Los Angeles and the "culture" in general. In the words of Black Flag, they are "damaged."

Pettibon links the idea of regeneration through sexual satisfaction to the idea of "regeneration through violence."[5] Manson

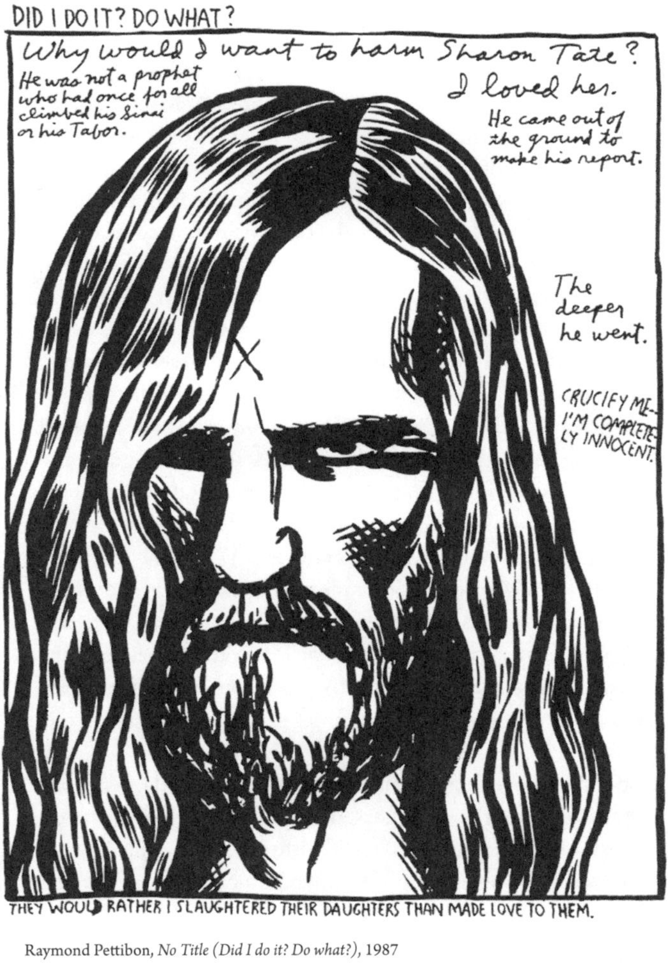

Raymond Pettibon, *No Title (Did I do it? Do what?)*, 1987

understood the psychology of this process. When he first made love to new members of the Family he would tell them to pretend he was their father. To Manson his true father was authority, the government, the judge, the jail: "My father is the jailhouse. My father is your system. [...] I am only a reflection of you. [...] But I know this: that in your hearts and your own souls, you are as much responsible for the Vietnam war as I am for killing these people."[6] The drawing on the cover of Pettibon's book *Other Christs* (1982) shows two hippie types and two straight-looking adults watching a Christ-like Manson figure being crucified on TV. The viewers all have halos over their heads; and the caption reads, "I'm glad to see someone from our group making it." Pettibon puts the cultists on a plane equivalent to religion, and also connects them to media worship and to Andy Warhol's famous statement about everyone achieving fifteen minutes of stardom. He shows "the Family," or any family, for that matter, thrilled to see their exploits talked about in the newspapers and on TV. Warhol never did a portrait of Manson because his portraits deal with heroes, or hero/victims: Marilyn Monroe, Kennedy's assassination, Elvis, an American Indian. Manson is too articulate, too much a twister of language, too effective, to be put up as an emblem of American culture.

The split between the romance of technology and its effects that erupted in the '60s, glossed over in the work of most Pop artists, was usurped by Robert Smithson. Now in the '80s Mike Kelley presents this unresolved situation again, but from

5 The phrase is taken from Richard Slotkin's essay "Dreams and Genocide: The American Myth of Regeneration through Violence," first published in *Journal of Popular Culture* (Summer 1971).

6 Quoted in Vincent Bugliosi (with Curt Gentry), *Helter Skelter: The True Story of the Manson Murders* (New York: W. W. Norton & Co., 1974).

a viewpoint of confusion rather than through Smithson's idea of gradual decay or entropy. Kelley is a performance artist who in the last couple of years has extended his work into the art gallery. Many of the props he uses in his performances have been shown in gallery installations. Additional paintings, drawings, and sculpture often deal with the same themes as the performances, but stand on their own as installations and as individual works. Imbued with a sense of energy and motion, they can be connected either directly to the performances themselves or to a sense of performing. Their tentative quality suggests that they are mementos of the artist's overall activity and ongoing thought process rather than precious objects unto themselves. In this way the artist is more powerful than the product.

Like Pettibon, Kelley uses the gesture of illustrative cartoons as an appropriated, ordinary form, and as a means by which to contrast extraordinary images. His playfully vulgar subject matter and juvenile sensibility make the postconceptual and structuralist influence on the work nearly invisible. He uses structuralist devices to make fun of the myth of rational thought which led to the myth of progress. Kelley creates a superstructure that shows the mechanics of nature to be as complex as the superstructure of technology. He points out that this seamless world of seeming perfection is in the hands of humans who are neither seamless nor perfect, allowing the possibility for anything to happen. Kelley's man, often the character he plays in his performances, has an overactive libidinous nature. As he tries to "control" his quest for "the sublime" the sacrificed emotions, finding no outlet for expression, build on themselves, eventually manifesting themselves in some taboo display which reduces him to a kind of monkey's ass.

Kelley's work is often associated with that of Jonathan Borofsky. The look of the artists' installations is similar, but the differences between them are enormous and significant. Because Kelley works up an actual juvenile energy, the world he creates is immoral, as opposed to Borofsky's moral order. Kelley's embarrassing takes are like Freud gone haywire. His swirling, pulsating lines create a sense of erotic fixation and project a horror and incestuous smothering not unlike that caused by Poe's houses of death, or, to give a more contemporary example, the movie *Alien*. In *Alien*, the being grows into a huge phallic monster which strangles and engulfs the spacemen; their technology is helpless against it. In a work entitled *Buried Treasure* (1983) Kelley illustrates reward and punishment. The piece consists of two drawings in a vertical diptych. The top drawing shows a treasure chest sitting in a hole, while the bottom drawing shows a hole filled with garbage. Around the top of the lower drawing is written (right side up), "Someone else's waste material"; written upside down along the bottom of the same drawing is the phrase "The reward comes only from strict adherence to directions." Around the edges of the treasure-chest drawing—beginning across the top and going down the side, along the bottom and up the other side—is a text that begins, "The right hole must be examined carefully to exhume the nugget of satisfaction-treasure." You have to twist your head upside down and sideways to follow the meandering text. Having done this you feel a little foolish, reduced to a lower state—like a dog digging a hole, following the scent of reward.

Tony Oursler is another artist who uses home-style animation and a childlike scrawl as a means of recapturing the viewer from the slick technological manipulation of the entertainment business. He works primarily in video and video installations,

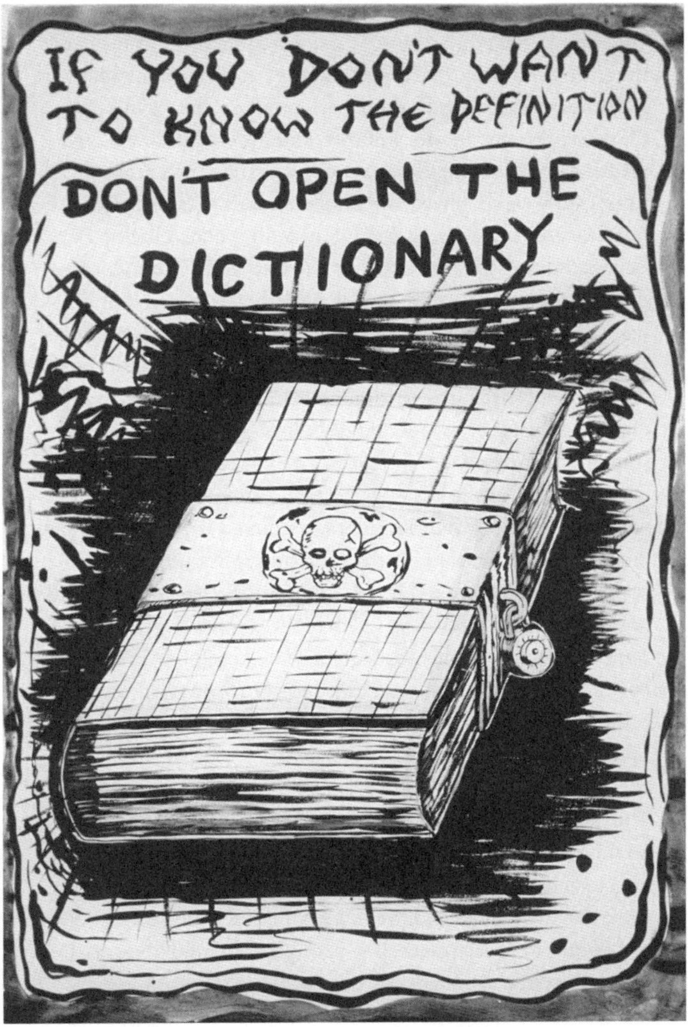

Mike Kelley, *If You Don't Want to Know the Definition Don't Open the Dictionary*, 1984

producing darkly humorous works. He begins by seducing the viewer with a lush and sensual array of sets. At times his narrations are the stories of the sets themselves as they collapse and metamorphose into something else. In *Spin Out* (1983–84), Oursler presents the story of man and his evolution into the future. One of the tape's sequences, a flashback to biblical times, shows a shepherd and his sheep on a hillside looking out peacefully at a starry night. Suddenly a constellation is delineated and changes first into the face of E.T., then into a demon, then into a good god, and finally into a god shedding tears for man. Oursler imitates the way the media manipulates and fabricates our past and future. Elsewhere his use of the soap-opera genre turns sentimentality into social parody. *Spin Out* literalizes the "suspended disbelief" that describes the state of the moviegoer who desperately wants to believe the experience he or she knows to be two-dimensional. Oursler's work, like Pettibon's and Kelley's, is imbued with detail, which contributes to its dramatically realistic quality. This modern realism used to be called science fiction. The moral at the end of the tape is that "nothing will happen to modern man." The puppet figure of man is absurdly not killed off. Just in the nick of time it is jerked away from disaster by a string. Among many other things, Oursler here is poking fun at America's religion of optimism.

The dark, obsessive edge that holds Oursler's tapes together could easily get lost in more formal concerns, as his work begins to achieve the seductive qualities of entertainment. However, Oursler's sense of life as a version of David Cronenberg's TV-paranoid *Videodrome* allows his work to hold to its critique. Recently Oursler showed one of his tapes at the New York club Danceteria. The tape was looped footage of two children, a boy and a girl, playing with plastic ray guns. For ten

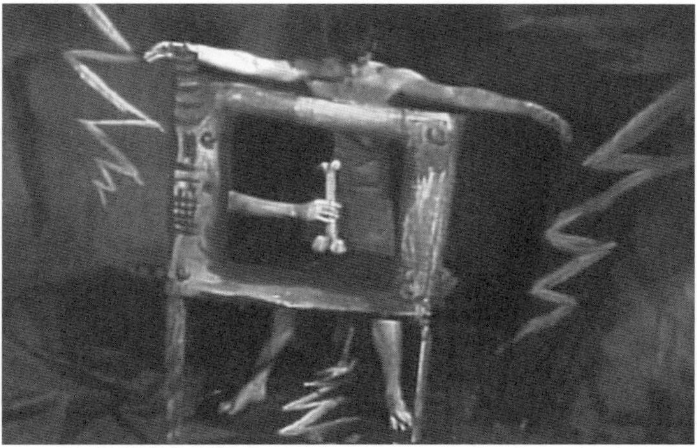

Tony Oursler, still from *EVOL*, 1984

minutes the sound of the toys blasted through the sci-fi-like, utopian environment of the club's video lounge, driving a lot of people out and symbolically killing off the '60s/'80s myth of the seamless relationship between popular culture and art. Most video and art shown at the club works only as ambient decoration. Oursler's new tape is titled *EVOL* (1984–85)—"love" spelled backward. The reference to the '60s is blatant.

The '60s manufactured an illusion of "here and now"; in the '80s truth passes into fiction and out again, history is recycled into the present without a context, and the present has become a leap of faith, as we sit back and enjoy the ultrafast life of MTV. In the '80s the art world has come to mirror the fast-food culture that Pop art ended up glorifying. In one way or another Pettibon, Kelley, and Oursler, with their psychedelic, seemingly expressionistic styles, connect this moment to the '60s to lead us back not for a nostalgic pondering, but for a confrontation with this crucial time.

By focusing on the split between the romance of technology and its forces of control they can isolate the manipulations that Pop art glossed over. Instead of producing ironic grand glossy icons to the products of popular culture, these artists are looking at its seamier sides. They do this by looking not down from above, but at themselves. Their use of male adolescent sexuality and the cartoon genre exaggerates and magnifies dynamics in human relationships not often visible in art, film, or TV. Their work belongs more to the literary tradition of Melville or Twain than to current figurative painting.

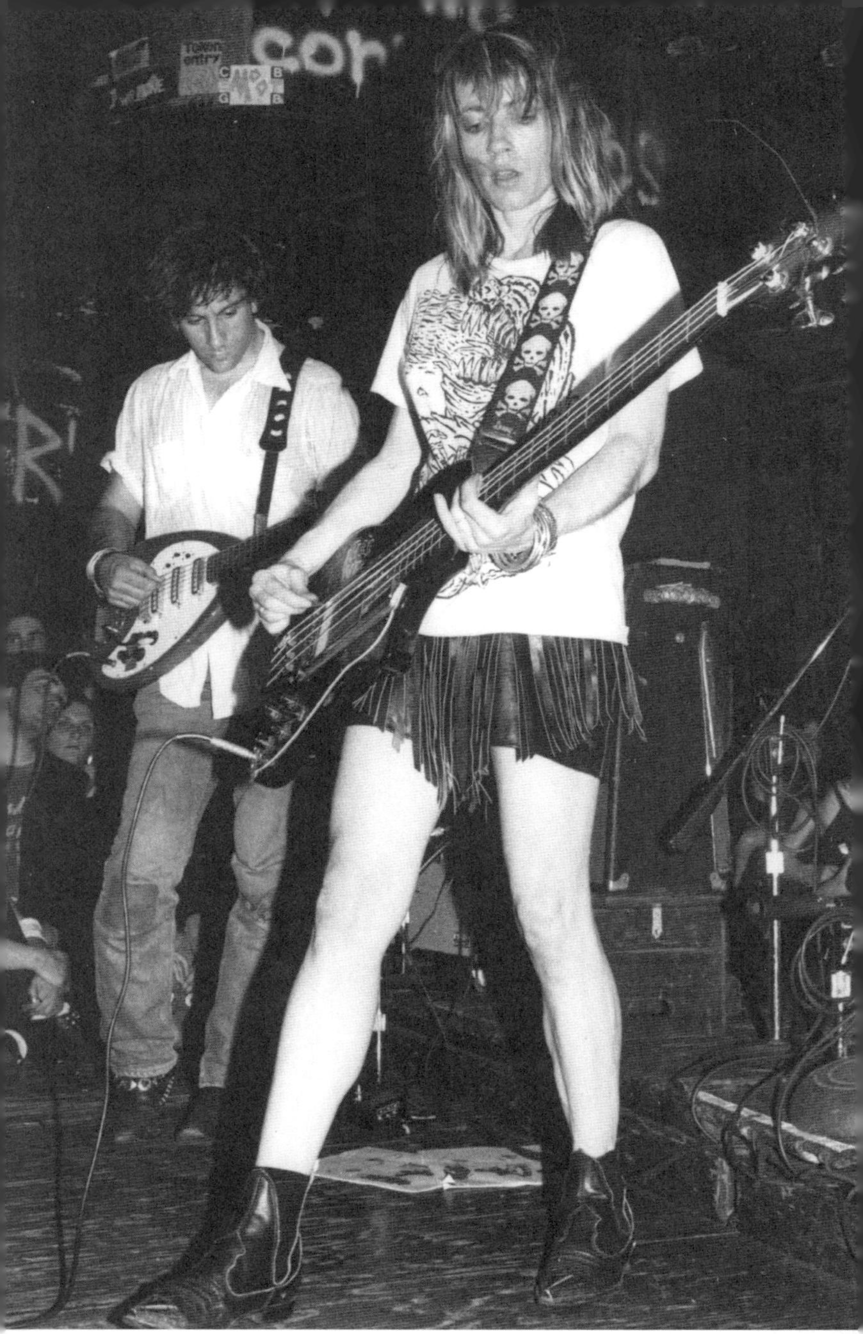

Boys Are Smelly: Sonic Youth Tour Diary, '87

Before picking up a bass I was just another girl with a fantasy. What would it be like to be right under the pinnacle of energy, beneath two guys crossing their guitars, two thunderfoxes in the throes of self-love and male bonding? How sick, but what desire could be more ordinary? How many grannies once wanted to rub their faces in Elvis's crotch, and how many boys want to be whipped by Steve Albini's guitar?

In the middle of the stage, where I stand as the bass player of Sonic Youth, the music comes at me from all directions. The most heightened state of being female is watching people watch you. Manipulating that state, without breaking the spell of performing, is what makes someone like Madonna all the more brilliant. Simple pop structures sustain her image, allowing her real self to remain a mystery—is she really that sexy? Loud dissonance and blurred melody create their own ambiguity—are we really that violent?—a context that allows me to be anonymous. For my purposes, being obsessed with boys playing guitars, being as ordinary as possible, being a girl bass player is ideal, because the swirl of Sonic Youth music makes me forget about being a girl. I like being in a weak position and making it strong.

We're the Archies!

People who can't even believe we have an audience are always curious about who they are. Maybe half the crowd who shows up in New York are *real* fans: noise buffs, death rockers, yuppies who have never heard a Sonic Youth record but know who

Originally published in the *Village Voice Rock & Roll Quarterly* (Fall 1988).

Left: Kim Gordon and Lee Ranaldo performing in Sonic Youth, 1986

Lydia Lunch is, rock writers, fanzine moguls, and sexual misfits, each and every one of them dressed in black. In LA everyone is more power-shag. In other cities audiences are younger, mostly fourteen- and fifteen-year-olds from areas that have cable (MTV's *120 Minutes*), get exposed to us, and, unlike college students, have nothing better to do. New Yorkers familiar with Sonic Youth never consider us a teeny-bopper band, but that just goes to show how provincial New Yorkers really are. They should get out of the city more often and see the world.

A lot has changed though since Sonic Youth began in '81. Cofounder and guitarist Thurston Moore named a show he was booking *Noisefest*. That's where we met guitarist Lee Ranaldo and the band came together. The festival's name was a joke, inspired by the owner of Hurrah who had said he was gonna close the club because all the bands just sounded like a bunch of noise. Nobody even knew what a noise band was. I wondered if people would be disappointed in Europe, the easiest place for New York bands to get gigs, because we didn't fit the image. Next to our friends the Swans, who were very loud and had a percussionist who pounded metal, we were total wimps.

Every Night, A Different Gig

Lyle Hysen, drummer for Das Damen, a New York band with a Deep Purple-like zest for guitar curdle and intricate song structures that frame a tragicomic persona (if comedian Richard Lewis were a band, they'd be it), told me about this vision he had that would change the face of indie rock. Instead of the band going on the road, from city to city, the audience would tour. For instance, they could do the Midwest. Head out to Minneapolis and see the Replacements, Soul Asylum, and Run Westy Run. Get back on the bus and drive to Madison for Killdozer, Die Kreuzen, and the Tar Babies. Just think, every night a different gig.

You'd be better off than the typical small touring band. There'd be no endless bickering about where-what-when to eat, all that draining decision-making. The tour manager would take care of everything, so you could just concentrate on watching the bands play. If the bus broke down, well, maybe you'd miss a gig, but it's *not your responsibility*.

Personally, I like to know that a band has suffered by the time they get onstage. Like the first time Redd Kross toured. Out of some thirty dates they did six. They drove out of LA in some crappy station wagon they bought with a record company advance, and they had big suitcases filled with their gear—high-heeled sneakers, spangled bell-bottoms, poly-coated blouses—and everything got all messy and wrinkled, but a half dozen times they shimmied onstage and played their hearts out.

Richmond, 9/14

I never feel like we're really on a tour 'till we hit Richmond. The wide streets feel different, slow and empty, and then I know we've left NYC/New Jersey/Philly/Baltimore/DC. That turnpike shit is the ugliest anywhere.

"Mom, I Gave the Cat Some Acid" was the funny industrial rock song by Happy Flowers we covered tonight when we played with them. They covered Sonic Youth's "Catholic Block" and wailed all over us, 'cause they're so fucking cute. There were a couple guys from Fishbone hanging out, trying to be funnier than anyone else. One guy was trying to impress me, telling me what neighborhood he comes from in LA. He said that he could be making a lot of money selling crack, but he preferred to play music. I really felt like saying to him, "Yeah, so fucking what, I'm a girl and here's my ghetto, pal."

Chapel Hill, 9/15

The Cat's Cradle was packed and too hot to remember anything. The last time we played in Chapel Hill, '82, it was the old Cat's Cradle, which was filled with the kind of dreariness that comes from redneck bars.

That was our first tour, us and the Swans. Yeah, we thought we were hot shit. (We had a record out and had played CBGB, the Mudd Club, and Danceteria.) It was raining and sad as hell, and the headlining Swans played their set to six jeering cowboys. Chapel Hill is one of the hippest places on earth to play, but in 1982 we were too underground or something. Mike Gira, the leader of the Swans, introduced a song amid giggles and chants for "Freebird" by saying, "This next song is about getting buttfucked by a cop," or something to that effect. We stood around waiting to see if Harry Crosby, then the English bass player for the Swans, who was as drunk as anyone, would feel the need to defend their honor. But nothing happened, a fitting end to a stupid evening.

All ten of us piled into the van, and the Swans fought among themselves. Morale was very low, tempers short, and our expectations not as high as Mike's, which is why they scream at one another. One night Mike and his drummer started strangling each other and calling each other "Dickhead" and "Asshole." Meanwhile everyone else is crammed around them trying to mind his or her own business, being really cool.

Atlanta, 9/16

On the drive from Athens to Atlanta there's this great snow-cone stand run by a six-year-old who offers a million different flavors—poppy seed or corn dog, for instance. We've totally given up on Athens, where we played twice and nobody came. The first time was the night Gira jumped off the stage and pushed someone who was pogoing. Mike thought the guy was a poser who was making fun of him. In reality he was a nerd, and Mike had never seen a nerd before.

We played at the Metroplex in Atlanta. As wholesome as Athens likes to think it is, Atlanta is self-consciously decadent. For instance, when my bass amp broke during the set, I felt pressured to go through the motions, pretending that sound was still blasting out, dry-humping as it were. Someone in the audience shouted, "Play some fucking noise, that's what it's all about isn't it? Stop complaining that the PA isn't loud enough." This is the kind of expert who will later review the show, complaining that no one stuck a drill up his butt.

Anyway, Atlanta used to have a super bad reputation as an evil punk scene, lots of kids hanging out and slashing the tires of touring bands, a real pit. Thurston tried to discourage his sister, Susan, from coming to the Metroplex. He must've thought we were gonna suck, or that he had to protect her. Thurston is really hung up about having to protect women, must be his upbringing. (Thurston and I even had a Catholic wedding.) He told Susan she'd be raped and murdered if she came. A handsome redhead, thirty, the mother of four, she ignored him and appeared at the club with a camera around her neck, gasping to their cousins, "God, I'm the only nerd here!" Someone asked Susan for her autograph.

We stayed at her house and awoke to food flying around the room and babies crawling all over us. I know many people think we indulge in twisted sex and ingest massive amounts of drugs on tour, and of course we do. But I'll always remember Susan, standing in the driveway with the kids and waving good-bye.

Texas, 9/17

On our way to Dallas, we just melt, sleep, and nag our drummer Steve Shelley about driving too slow and Thurston for driving too much like he plays guitar. Lee Ranaldo is holding his movie camera out the window again, and Terry Pearson our soundman is ripping thru another rock 'n' roll autobiography. He can read one in ten minutes. Suzanne Sasic is also with us.

Suzanne is our T-shirt vendor and runs the lighting board. Tomboyish, but with long red hair, she wears spurs and keeps her money in her boots. Her penchant for wearing glitter and silver, combined with her almost translucent skin, are other reasons we call her our goddess of light. Suzanne and I sit in the last row of the van and complain about something or other or just voice our opinions in general. No one ever listens to us. It's so far back, what with the windows open and stereo blasting, that we have to shout to be heard. "Turn that shit off." "Stop the car, I have to pee." Thurston complains that we're always mumbling.

Suzanne has a diet that's a challenge to accommodate. She won't eat anything green, except guacamole, and will only eat *the middle* of various foods like pancakes and cheese omelettes. (She hates the egg part.) Spaghetti, chocolate, and orange juice are staples. I'm writing this as a warning for all the boys across the country who write to ask who the vixen with the devastating eyes is. Does she care? No, she's a heartbreaker. Just send obscure vinyl, After Eights, and forget the rest.

Buffalo, 5/9
There are these kids here—the Neurotic Family Production Company—who have an inscribed cake ("SONIC LIFE") made for us every time we play one of their shows. Last time we played there with Das Damen, and they're going, "You guys suck, I can't believe they made you a cake."

The nicer the promoter, the better the food, the worse the gig is usually, except New York gigs, which don't need any reason to suck. Our shows in Europe tend to be less exciting for this reason.

Switzerland, 6/9
Misjudging the drive from Paris, we're about six hours late for a live radio broadcast at one of those state-of-the-art radio stations. I like to think it was Carlos's fault, our booking agent/tour manager in Europe. Carlos is a tall, gangly, soft-spoken friend of ours who came into the job of booking bands through social work. (Holland gives government subsidies to its rock clubs.) When we're together our stereotypes of one another become more pronounced; he is the self-righteous, hard-working, Dutch manager, and we're the spoiled, self-centered, American rock assholes. In Europe, we're almost always late. In America we're pretty self-sufficient.

The most fun thing about having Carlos around is listening to the way he tries to shame us. "I don't want to, I don't want to," he'll say, rolling his head from side to side. He has met or heard about every wasted performer on the European circuit, and he still thinks we're bad when we want to stop for bangles and candy. We find it essential to stop everywhere to exercise our right as Americans to spend freely. To tour is to shop. This drives Carlos crazy.

Anyway, we get to the radio station in Geneva very late, but they still want us to play, which is unfortunate. Carlos is disappointed in our attitude. We started complaining about having to do the show when we found out we weren't getting paid. And it's the same old story about how we'll end up with a high quality live recording, but we already know it's gonna be lame because it's a dead room and we'll be playing in front of five Swiss people bobbing their heads and smiling politely.

So of course they have a great spread of pâté, cheeses, and smoked ham. We feel like slobs surrounded by this plush equipment and stark beige environment, quiet as a bomb shelter. From the first note it's a disaster. Thurston starts whispering obscenities over the intro to "Cotton Crown." We feel like jerks, so pretty soon Thurston is swearing new lyrics to all the songs, and no one stops us. (Some of this session did end up on the B-side of *Master=Dik.*)

Switzerland was the only place I ever had my ass bitten by someone in the audience. I'd turn my back, and the guy would jump out and bite me, and I'd have to fight him off. When he kept doing it Thurston kicked a glass in his face. It really destroyed the mood.

Boston, 10/18

There was a point when I started getting sickened by the violence onstage. Thurston's fingers would swell up all purple and thick from banging his guitar. Usually I never know what's happening onstage, I would just see guitar-like objects whizzing through the air out of the corner of my eye. A couple of times Thurston pushed Lee into the audience, as the only way to end a song, but that was harmless fun.

At our first gig in Boston about four years ago, *Conflict* editor Gerard Cosloy, *Forced Exposure*'s Jimmy Johnson, and this idiot fan named Billy were just about the only ones there. During the first song Billy picked up this broken drumstick that had flown onto the floor and threw it back. It speared into my forehead. At first I thought it had bounced off Thurston's guitar. Shocked, I didn't know whether to cry or keep playing, but then I just felt incredibly angry. It took a long time to resolve that incident, 'cause it really made me feel sick, violated, like walking to the dressing room after a set, having some guy say, "Nice show," then getting my ass pinched as I walk away.

I blamed it on the music for a while, because it did draw fans who really want to see you hurt yourself. It's not that I don't share similar expectations; there's beauty in things falling apart, in the dangerous (sexual) power of electricity, which makes our music possible. But what was once a hazy fantasy has since clarified itself. I don't want my blood to be entertainment.

When we most recently played the Channel in Boston, some kid threw a handful of firecrackers in my face. I threw down my bass and left the stage, and so did the rest of the band. We figured out what happened and went back on to finish the set, while the bouncers were throwing the kid out. I was actually beginning to feel sorry for him, probably a misplaced Aerosmith fan.

Naugatuck, Connecticut, 10/24

There's nothing like Naugatuck on a Saturday night. It was just about the last gig on the tour. The club is next to a Chinese restaurant in a shopping plaza. *River's Edge* could have been filmed here. I've never seen so many metalheads cruising the roads. They make perfect sense, though, when you look at the barren trees, the discount store, all this desolation and quietness—you want to crank up something really loud and ugly. I couldn't help wondering what the girls did while the boys were off playing with Satan. Maybe they also crave electricity, swirling around their heads, through their legs.

I know what they feel like. When Iggy Pop came onstage in Naugatuck (or was it London?) to sing "I Wanna Be Your Dog," Lee and Thurston were ready to rock. I was amazed that he was so professional. He expressed the freakiness of being a woman and an entertainer. I felt like such a cream puff next to him. I didn't know what to do, so I just sort of watched.

Secret Message

This guy writes me letters. He tells me up front he's been hospitalized for mental disturbances several times and asks that I stop sending messages to him through our music. Guys like this take over your whole life if you give them even a smidgen of attention. So if you read this, baby, stop sending those letters.

The original, unedited typescript of the Naugatuck section (reproduced in the catalogue for "Sensational Fix") further develops Gordon's observations on gender and performance:

There's nothing like playing Naugatuck, Conn., on a Saturday night. It was just about the last gig on the tour. The club is in a shopping plaza, next to a Chinese restaurant. I think that about says it all. If you saw the movie *River's Edge* and liked it then you'll like Naugatuck. I've never seen so many teen metalheads (Satan?) cruising the roads in one small town before. It makes perfect sense though when you look at all the barren trees with the red fall leaves all over the ground and then you look around at the discount store in the shopping plaza and it makes you want to crank up something really loud and ugly to forget this desolation and quietness. I couldn't help wondering what the girls did while the boys were off playing with Satan. And I wondered if they were like me and craved the feeling of electricity and sound mixed together, swirling around my head and thru my legs. I always fantasized what it would be like to be right under the pinnacle of energy, beneath two guys who have crossed their guitars together, two thunder foxes in the throes of self-love and combat, that powerful form of intimacy only achieved on stage in front of other people, known as male bonding. How sick, but what could be more mundane and ordinary a desire, but isn't that what it boils down to. How many grannies wanted to rub their faces in Elvis's crotch and how many boys wanted to be buttfucked by Steve Albini's guitar? In the middle of the stage, where I stand, the music comes at me from all directions. The most cultivated state of being female is watching other people watch you, which makes all women natural voyeurs and someone like Madonna all the more brilliant, but not necessarily a desirable position to attain. For my purposes, being obsessed with boys playing guitars, being as ordinary as possible, like being a girl bass player is, in a sense ideal. The only time I actually felt like an outsider on stage is when Iggy Pop came onstage to sing, "I Wanna Be Your Dog." Lee and Thurston felt pretty much at home with this, whereas I felt, wow he's taking my place, cause I usually sing this song, I mean it is his song and all, but it didn't have to do with him being so much more well known and idolized and all, but it's just that he is such a freak, it's not like Mick Jagger or someone like that pretending to be freaky by being womanish and strutting around. Leave it to a man, the Ig, to express the freakiness of being a woman better than she can. I felt like such a creampuff next to the real thing. This image shot into my head of Jagger and Tina Turner doing a duet together on TV for some benefit, and god that was disgusting, the more professional about it they were the more sickening it appeared. I don't have any role models, I didn't know what to do so I just sort of watched.

FAMA & FORTUNE FANZINE

Kim Gordon

Mike Kelley

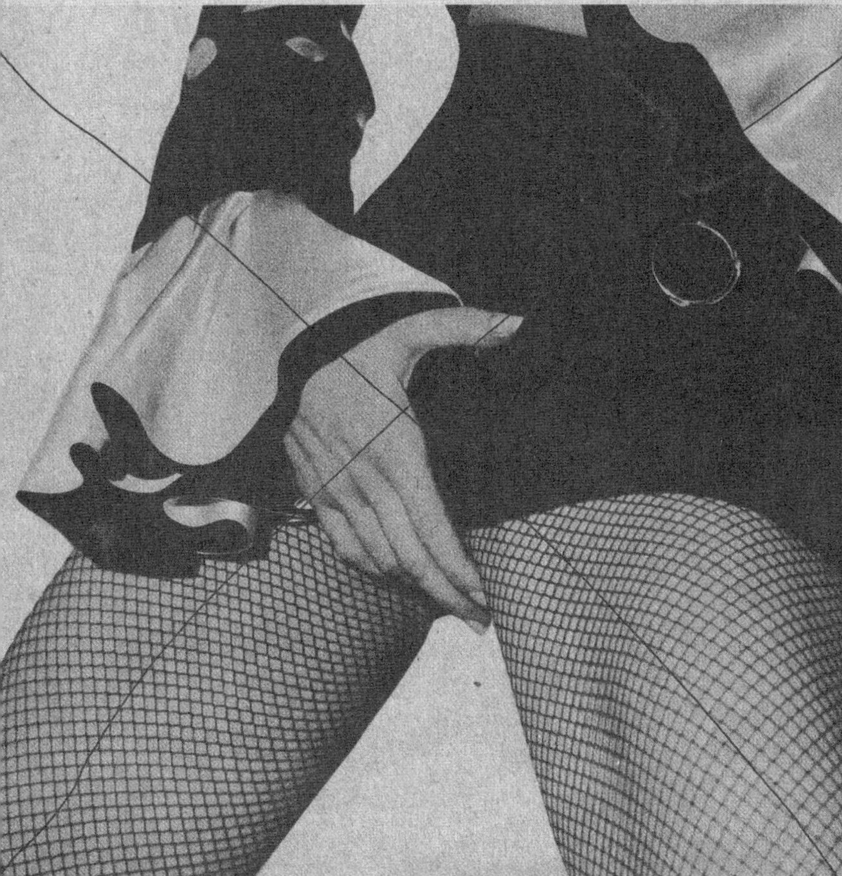

P&S Wien

November 1991 / 8

Forget M/M, K/T Is the Trip

I met Kim Gordon in the late '70s when she was still a California girl, still an artist, and still a "librarian type." Now Kim's the hot and steamy female member of Sonic Youth.

Kim Gordon of Sonic Youth in New York interviewed by Mike Kelley in Los Angeles via telephone.

Mike Kelley: This is Mike Kelley, and I'm talking to Kim Gordon. Go ahead. Talk.

Kim Gordon: Hello.

MK: Hello. I am calling representing *Interview* magazine.

KG: Well, I hope you're getting paid well. *(laughing)*

MK: I think so. I want to focus on you—more on you—and then we'll talk about Sonic Youth. But the first question I'm going to ask is about your transformation recently into a sex symbol. How do you see that? I know from talking to kids that you're considered hot stuff.

KG: Really?

MK: Yeah. For instance, I read an interview in a music magazine not long ago with a member of Big Black and he had this huge fantasy about sniffing your underpants and so on.

KG: He's always trying to get attention.

Originally published in *Fama & Fortune Bulletin*, no. 8 (November 1991).
All images are from the original publication.

MK: It seems funny considering that until recently your image was that of the smart girl, the behind-the-scenes organizer, or the art link in the band—something like that. Now, especially in the video for the song "Kool Thing," which is getting television play, you're the steamy front girl. How do you see your transformation? Especially since it's something that's happened to you as an adult, not as a teenager.

KG: Well, it's odd, because when I was twelve or thirteen my mother was so *afraid* for me, because I apparently just—you know, oozed sexuality. I looked older than my age. She was such a prude, and she was always saying—oh, you know, "Read books," and "Boys won't respect you." I was virtually a tomboy, though. Sexuality was ingrained as being *bad*. And then when I started getting involved with art seriously, I just got really ugly. *(laughing)* I started wearing glasses when I was twenty and—

MK: Right. Going for the librarian look. But you were never ugly.

KG: Yeah. Well fashion was something that was just beyond me. My idols were mostly male guitarists.

MK: Were they your sex symbols? Did you leave art to chase after rock gods?

KG: I didn't really see male guitarists as sex symbols. But it was this kind of feeling—and I guess it's sort of a teenage thing, when you like a song—you want to play it over and over again. That was something that I couldn't find an equivalent to in art. It's very hard to get hot over a painting. You can have *crushes*. I definitely had crushes on art. But, still, there's no real equivalent in the art would for that teenage thing of obsessiveness. Maybe I'm wrong. Is there?

MK: I think when young people become obsessed with an artwork, they see it as ideology. It's not something that picks them up and moves them physically. It's more mental, more repressed.

KG: Right. But an ideology can be sexy in a way.

MK: That's similar. In both art and rock music ideology can be made sexy. Though I think it's easier in music to dispense with the ideology.

KG: I just don't do visual art anymore. My body's my canvas. *(laughing)*

MK: Yeah! A body artist!

KG: Clothes have become a visual outlet for me. I see this as a gradual transformation for me. Like doing the video for "Kool Thing" (which is a song about a girl singing about and to her favorite pop star) and dressing up in all these clothes I've acquired. To me, I'm a pseudo-sex symbol. Doing the video shows that anyone can do it. You utilize it—put it on for a moment and use it.

MK: Do you think that in relation to the band, becoming more of a visual identity was a way to work against the '70s cliché of the girl bass player—the Talking Heads syndrome.

KG: I find that really annoying. I suppose that's one reason for wanting to do more. Not only do you worry about being typecast as the token girl, but it's the token girl in the background playing the bass. One of the lamest interviews I ever did was with this girl from a San Francisco magazine called *Bitch*. She was like: "So, you're not like the lead singer or anything, so I guess you're sort of a Tina Weymouth type."

MK: Grrr!

KG: I just wanted to knock her silly. The main thing, I guess, is letting one's personality actually come through, not to become someone else—Marilyn Monroe, or Madonna, or whatever.

MK: Do you think that the Harry Crews tour and record was another way of establishing your identity outside of Sonic Youth and outside of those roles?

KG: It's a way of seeing myself differently. When you start a band like Sonic Youth everyone has their own role and to change that role is very hard. But in Harry Crews I was ultimately responsible, or felt I was, for how the music sounded. And I don't think of myself as a musician, so that was a really different role for me.

MK: Lydia Lunch has a reputation for being willful. On record it sounds as if you have to fight to interrupt her monologues. Was that situation about putting yourself in a position of having to assert yourself?

KG: Lydia was like—you know, anything you want to do—*right!* (*laughing*) When we started performing I had forgotten what Lydia's audience is like. They do only want to hear her say the word "fuck." And especially in Europe, where swear words translate so well. They're there for *that*. It was a miscal-

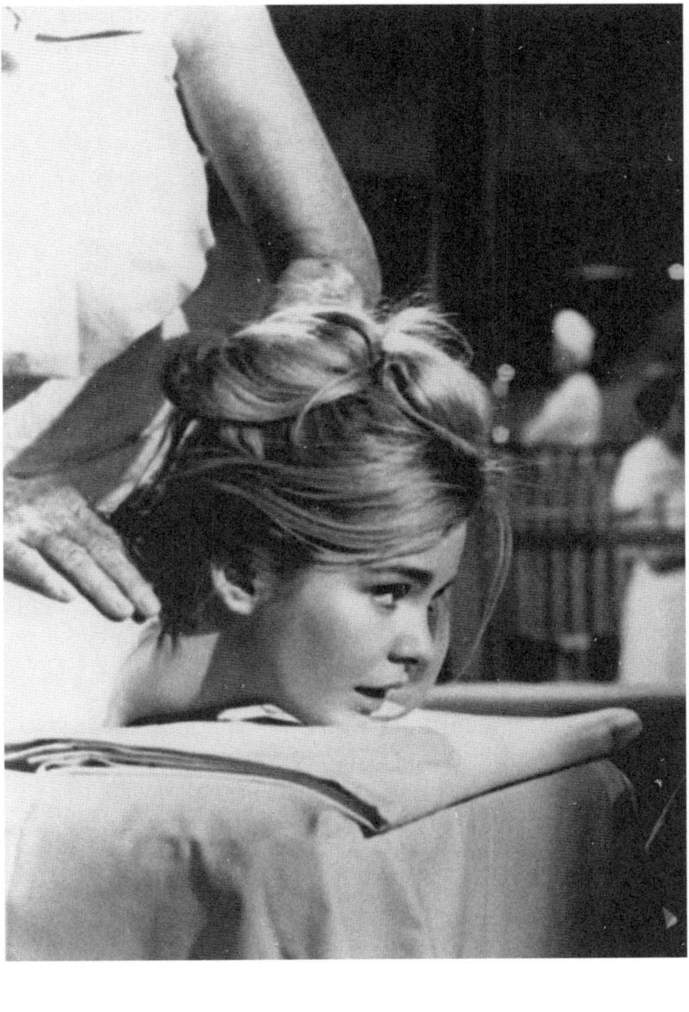

culation on my part. Thurston saw one of the gigs and said it looked like one side of the stage was performance art, Lydia's side, and the other side was music.

MK: Getting back to the mixture of ideology and rock, I always think of Sonic Youth as a band whose image is a surface of ideology—kind of harkening back to—almost a '60s idea of rock as representing some sort of—

KG: Free spirit?

MK: Well, some sort of rebellion. A lot of the songs have social edges. Say, the "Kool Thing" video really made me think about radical chic—of how at one point the Black Panthers were made into sex symbols. And also the name Sonic Youth—youthful rebellion as timeless—I mean, the band isn't made up of kids.

KG: I don't think we really believe in any ideology.

MK: I guess I'm talking more about an aura.

KG: To me the strength of the band has come from working intuitively and organically. Which is a way that, in music today, is very hard to do because people are so self-conscious. They're so media-aware. Working in that way was something that in the '60s, I think, people were able to do because it was all unexplored territory. The youth market hadn't been so co-opted. When we started as a band, New York City worked for us. It was sort of a haven, almost a shelter from the rock mainstream and the media because it really *was* cut off. In the early '80s we didn't know how to make records, it was like improv. I think that helped us. Maybe it's the same for kids who are out in the suburbs. Even though—we're so *urban*—you think New York is urban and it's the center of media, but in a way New York is cut off from the mainstream music world. You don't even get MTV if you live downtown. I think that enabled us to, almost from memory, take from what we grew up listening to—kind of like we were *approximating* rock.

MK: Who do you think your audience is?

KG: I have no idea. I mean it's different in different parts of the country. I think the Midwest tends to be really young, and—you know, I don't really know. Audience-shmaudience. *(laughing)* I don't know who our audience is.

MK: It's funny that you talk of being cut off from the mainstream of rock when on your new album, *Goo*, you have certain kinds of songs that point toward that kind of rock—rock in the populist mode. You have a road song and you have a marriage song. I particularly thought that having a road song was funny, it reminds me of Grand Funk Railroad or something, a self-reflexive song about the nomadic life of the rock star.

KG: That's interesting. On this record the songs stand more on their own as separate things, more so than on the last record where there was more of a total mood. There's a song on *Goo* called "Tunic" which is about Karen Carpenter, and it reminds me somewhat of the Shangri-Las. This is probably the closest I'll ever get to doing the Shangri-La talking song.

MK: What's the relationship of Ciccone Youth to all this?

KG: None really. Actually, that record was recorded before the last Sonic Youth record, *Daydream Nation*. It just ended up coming out afterwards. When we decided to do the Ciccone Youth we didn't plan it as a hip-hop record, though it's been seen that way. We had done a cover version, "Into the Groovey," a year before that and we wanted to go into the studio and work with drum machines, without having any expectations—just being indulgent. We are more interested in German electronic rock of the late '70s like Neu! and Can than hip-hop.

MK: The Ciccone Youth record sounds quite a bit like that actually.

KG: It's more—you know, white groove oriented. We wanted to make some kind of change in the pattern before we started writing songs for *Daydream Nation*. In a way too much importance has been put on the Ciccone Youth record.

MK: Well, I think one of its attractions has to do with the aura of Madonna around the thing. (Ciccone is Madonna's real last name.)

KG: It's so different from the stuff we'd done as Sonic Youth that we thought it would confuse people too much, so we had to establish this other identity. We could have used any name, and maybe we should have. I don't know if we'll do more stuff like that. Probably not.

MK: A lot of people really like that record.

KG: A friend of mine said it was the most evil record he'd ever heard. *(laughing)* He regarded it as—you know, sort of a Satan teen record or something.

MK: So, what about titling the new album *Goo*?

139 FORGET M/M, K/T IS THE TRIP

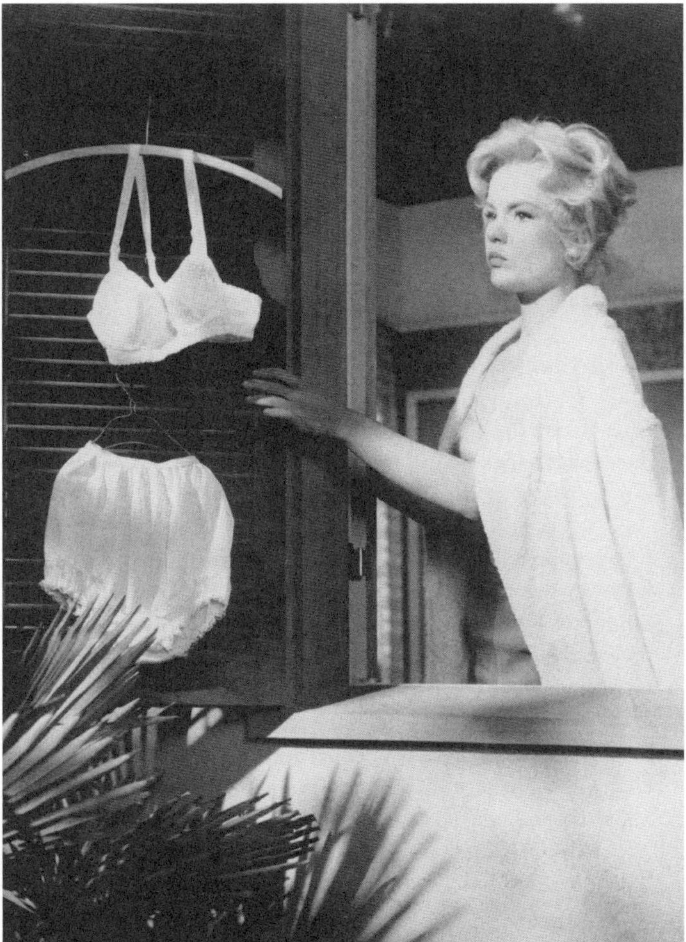

KG: We like the idea of people in the field-sales branches selling—*Goo*.

MK: *Goo*!

KG: You know—“How many *Goo*s would you like?”

MK: How would you respond to people who have trouble with the “Kool Thing” videotape, in the way blacks were used in it? Have you gotten any trouble from that?

KG: In what way? The interracial thing, or that it’s exploitive?

MK: Where the blacks are depicted as cultural others, as sexy dangerous things. I could see some people in the black community having trouble with that.

KG: I suppose black people could see that tape and say: “That is the way white people see us—as objects.” We were very careful to make sure that everyone looked good—the way they were photographed. It was deliberate that there were a lot of angles, like when the camera was down low, looking up at the black dude making him look regal. It has disturbed me that, in reviews of the song, people don’t get that I am not talking to Chuck D (Chuck D is a member of the rap group *Public Enemy*; he makes a minor vocal appearance in the song “Kool Thing”), but that I’m talking to a third person. Chuck D is just there as himself—reinforcing what I’m saying.

MK: Did Chuck D see the tape?

KG: I don’t know if he’s actually seen the tape. Probably not. He’s a busy man. But if the song makes people feel uncomfortable or question anything, I think that's good—even if they do misconstrue it. I wanted it to be ambiguous as to who was saying "I don't want to" in the song. Was it the girl, or was it the guy saying, "I don't want anything to do with you, white bitch." One of the problems with the video is how do you keep things ambiguous.

MK: It tends to break things down into particular roles.

KG: What do you think of the idea of women using their bodies as sex symbols to gain control? Do you think that's an illusion? Like Madonna, for instance.

MK: I think people use what they have access to.

KG: But don't you think that her whole life is geared to making herself the Madonna person? How can she have any time left to think another thought?

MK: I have to respect Madonna as a businesswoman, but I don't respect the aesthetic.

KG: She's a businesswoman in a man's world. What's the difference if a woman does it? Have you heard about her new tour where the men wear pointed bras?

MK: Well, I like that. That's funny, and I like that she does the Michael Jackson crotch grab.

KG: Do you think that is Madonna at her best?

MK: Yes, the theatrics.

KG: More and more she reminds me of a freak—you know, a Harry Crews (the writer) character. I know that she likes Harry Crews's writing but I don't know if she's been consciously influenced by his characters.

MK: I like that she's become sort of a female transvestite, that's kind of a contradiction of terms. Duh! Madonna! I don't know what all the stink's about. What brought her up? *(laughing)* Oh! Your question about women using their bodies to get control.

KG: My theory is that women make natural anarchists, because they are outside of the system in many ways. Like Tuesday Weld, early Tuesday Weld is sort of—

MK: *She's* my idol!

KG: That's what I would mean by "anarchist"—the unpredictable white female.

MK: Since you brought up Harry Crews the writer I want to get back to Harry Crews the band. I have a hard time believing the record liner notes which imply that the tour was supposed to promote literacy. Come on! *(laughing)* That's a lot to swallow—that a grungy female power trio will provoke its audience to read more. Was that tour an attempt to please your mother?

KG: It was particularly funny since we only toured in foreign countries.

MK: Could they understand what you were taking about?

143 FORGET M/M, K/T IS THE TRIP

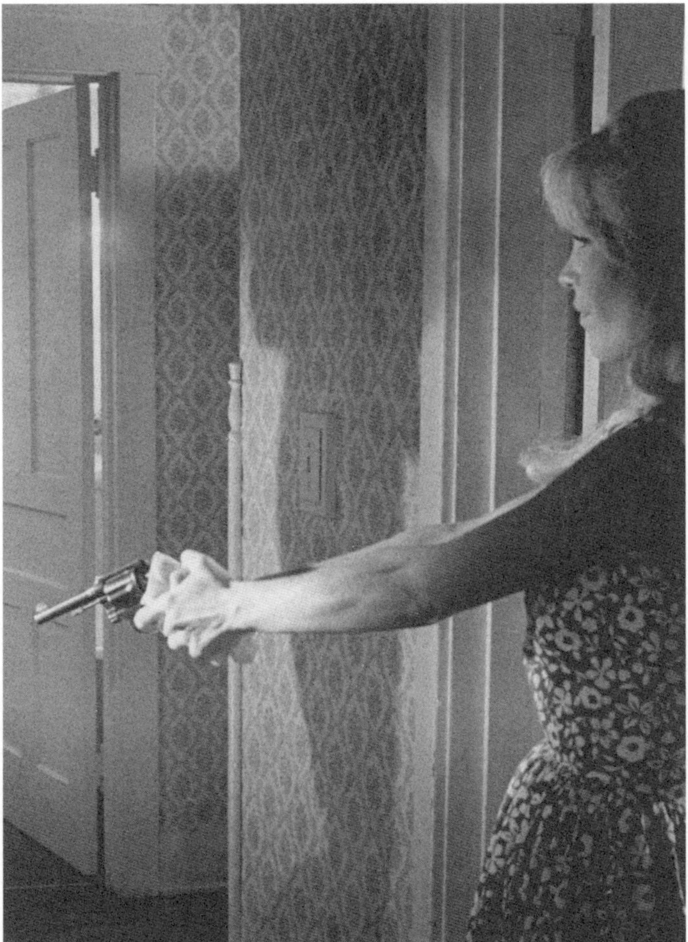

KG: Maybe, but they had never heard of the writer Harry Crews.

MK: As if they are going to care about perverse American hillbilly culture.

KG: It's exotica. … Do you think that's enough interview?

MK: I guess so.

KG: OK.

MK: All righty.

KG: See ya.

MK: Bye.

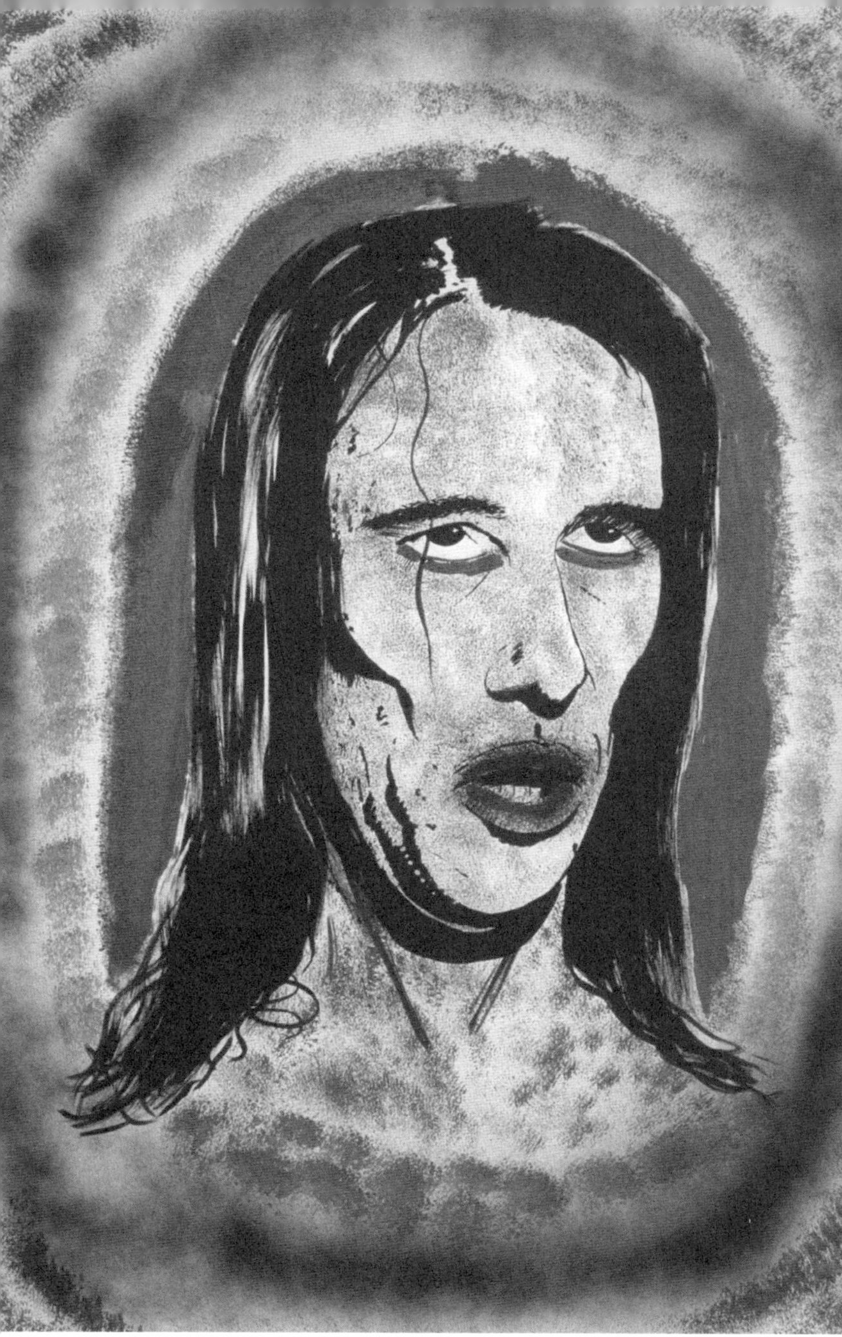

Is It My Body?

What have I got
That makes you want to love me?
Is it my body?
Or someone I might be?
Something inside me?
You better tell me. Tell me.
It's really up to you.
Have you got the time to find out
Who I really am?
What does it take
To get inside of your mind?
Give me a break, yeah, yeah,
And take a chance for the very first time.
You better tell me. Tell me.
It's really up to you
Have you got the time to find out
Who I really aaaaaaaam?

These lyrics for the song "Is It My Body" by Alice Cooper may well be some of the best rock lyrics ever written.[1] Originally from Phoenix, Arizona, Alice Cooper and his band moved to Detroit, where they were influenced by the heavy, high-energy Detroit sound of the Stooges et al.—a sound that was raw, primal, and noisy, with lyrics that gave a voice to white, confused teenage kids who felt alienated from their sexual identity.

1 "Is It My Body," words and music by Alice Cooper, Michael Bruce, Glen Buxton, Dennis Dunaway, and Neal Smith, © 1971 Bizarre Music Inc. and Alive Enterprises (BMI).

Originally published in the catalogue to the exhibition "Mike Kelley: Catholic Tastes," organized by Elisabeth Sussman, Whitney Museum of American Art, New York, 1993.

Left: Mike Kelley, study for *The Orange and Green*, 1989, from *Pansy Metal/Clovered Hoof*

This was quite different from the psychedelic sounds of California and the hippie rebellion. This was music coming out of disenchantment with the '60s.

1969 … the dregs, the end of utopia. Influences on the scene in Detroit were the sexual freaks (Iggy Pop, Alice Cooper), the race riots, and concerts featuring the MC5, the Art Ensemble of Chicago, Archie Shepp, and Sun Ra. There was much more of a white and black subculture crossover than existed in any other part of the country. This is the place where Mike Kelley comes from.

When I first saw Mike Kelley perform he had, as he does now, a wiry, electrified, androgynous presence. His gestures were both vaudevillian and rock and roll. Alice Cooper had taken androgyny in rock furthest by giving himself a woman's name and wearing garish makeup with glam and glitter stage clothes. He exemplified the blurring and the confusion being expressed in rock and roll. I can remember in high school so many kids at first wondering whether Alice Cooper was male or female. We could not believe that Alice was maybe a transvestite. Or a woman. Alice was so much more confusing than David Bowie, Marc Bolan, or Mick Jagger. The question lingered, "Was it a sex change?" We were far too repressed to come to any conclusions; they were all too horrifying. Except that it was just rock and roll, make-believe.

Mike used to play drums in an experimental noise rock band in Ann Arbor called Destroy All Monsters. Later, in art school, he played with a band called the Poetics. I don't think Mike ever imagined his artwork would someday travel around the world in the guise of a rock band's cover art. When Sonic Youth chose Mike's series of stuffed animal portraits (the piece entitled *Ahh ... Youth!,* as it appeared in *XXIst Century Magazine*) for the artwork on our 1992 CD *Dirty,* we knew it would work visually. But we hadn't anticipated the charismatic, E.T.-like emotional quality that the front cover image came to possess.

Up close, in person, they were dirty, missing parts. But on a glossy CD booklet they were suddenly stars. No longer were they simply mug shots. They were now mugging and adorably "grungy" against a pristine white square, each animal its own page. Most people who buy the CD don't realize that the images were and are part of a work of art. They always wanted to know the identity of the adolescent with bad skin whose photograph appears inside. We decided to include this photo of Mike as a teenager, probably for the same reason he included it within the series of stuffed animal portraits—to give some hint to the actual meaning of the word "dirty." Or rather, so that the viewers would be able to project themselves upon the images. If the two came face to face in a gallery, the dirty aspect would be a turnoff. Especially viewed within the same context as the photo Mike composed of the naked man and woman using stuffed animals as fetish objects. This was Mike's biggest selling show and these were probably the most expensive adult fetish objects ever made. We placed this "dirty" photo under colored plastic inside the CD jewel-case. This edition of the CD was limited to fifty thousand copies in the US (because of packaging costs ... or so they say). We wanted the photo to be included wherever possible because we didn't want the audience to think we were simply into what could be considered kitsch.

On our *Dirty* tour we had a merchandise booth where we sold stuffed animals that were bought from local Salvation Army shops and thrift stores. We pinned badges on the stuffed

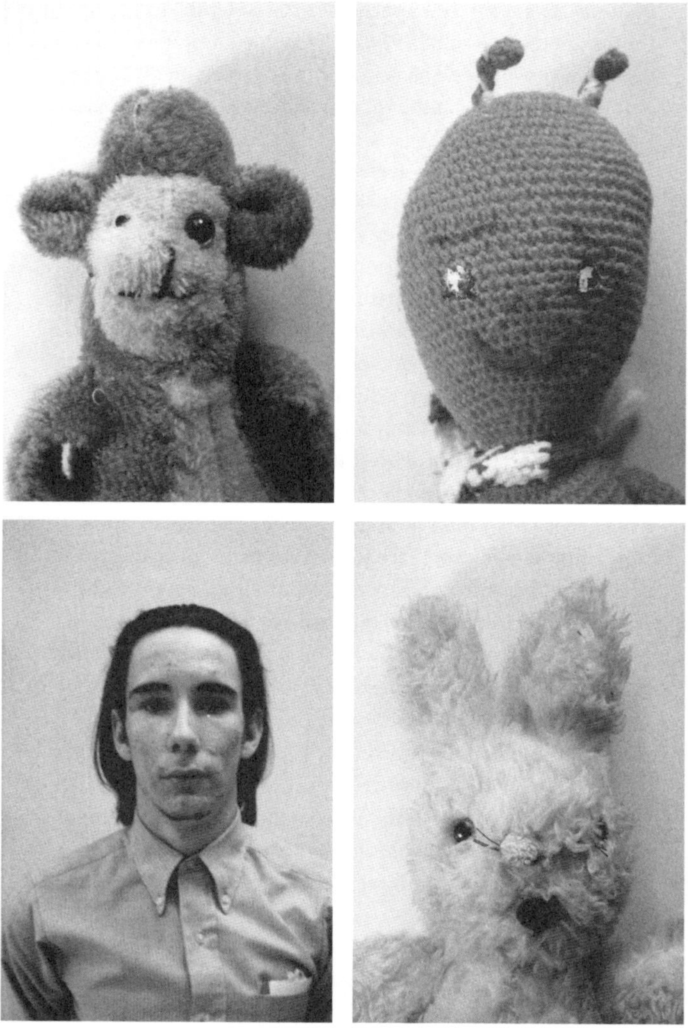

Mike Kelley, *Ahh … Youth!*, 1991

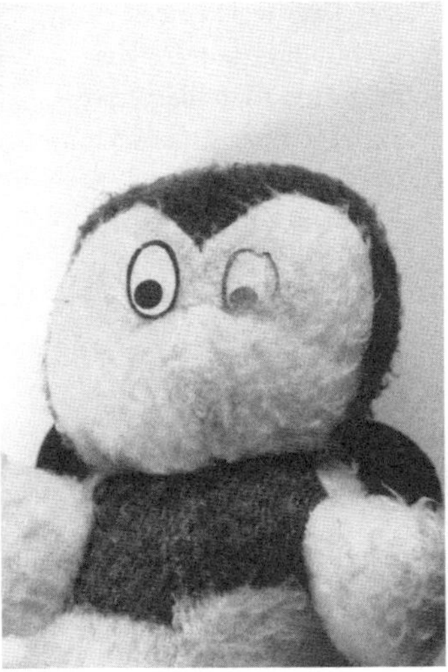
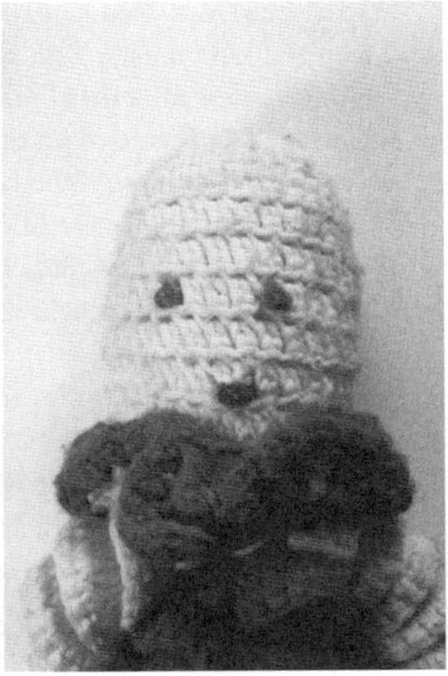
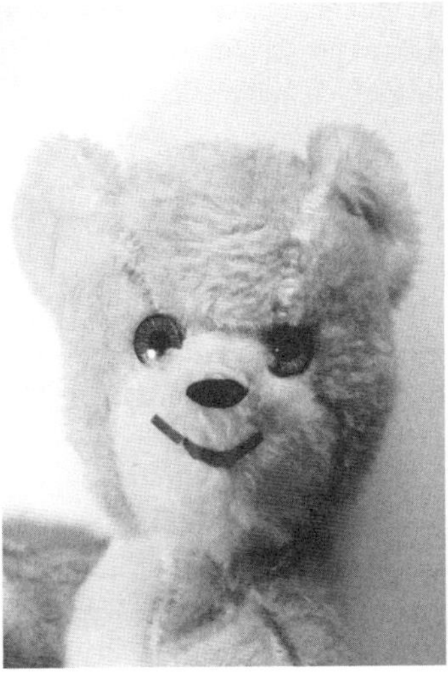
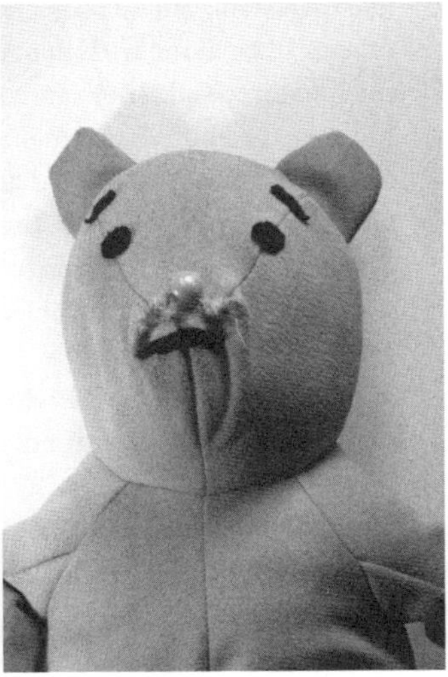

animals that read, "Hug me, I'm Dirty." They were priced really cheap and kids, mostly girls, probably bought them because as concert souvenirs they looked cute, rather than like depressing, used, and discarded pieces of synthetic fiber. Of course, it's possible they bought them because they liked Mike Kelley's artwork ... scary. Mike's stuffed animals work so well within the context of the rock genre because they are the perfect symbols for post-teenage rebellion.

This is a genre where aggression is acted out in an ultimately safe environment. Even the scariest heavy metal band has cartoon lyrics about Satan and hell. Puppet imagery is very common. Metallica's album *Master of Puppets* has an S/M implication as well as a reference to his lordship Satan. An even more repressed meaning concerns the relationship of the animals themselves to the audience. Mike Kelley's animals, like rock stars, can be projected upon. The real sexual power of rock stars, along with their imagined power, influences how they're perceived. They often appear much taller when performing. The body's not theirs anymore, it's a public domain and public perception. Michael Jackson is someone who has lost sight of his own body: the nose getting smaller, the skin lighter. As if he were trying to become a doll modeled after himself, a more abstract image of himself. The stuffed animal is already an abstract shape. Its dirty orange-and-red-colored yarn face blown up in the window displays of Tower Records stores cannot help but stimulate.

It's obvious that people like to project themselves onto stuffed animals. But the disheveled, orphan-like, androgynous "victim" or the "let me take you home and you can tie me up you wild and freaky thing" quality of the *Dirty* CD cover "art puppet" (many people call it this) mimics the classic male rock persona.

As long as sexual identity is blurred or played with, sexuality in rock can be dirty and still be unthreatening … romanticized.

Rock music is all about repression. Rap music, however, can be all about bragging about how male you are and can be. There is nothing ambiguous about it. When the lyrics are dirty it's considered, in some parts of the country, to be pornographic and/or obscene. The music is all about refusing to be repressed.

The "dirty" photo by Mike Kelley is shocking because we see a naked man and a naked woman doing something unconventional. They're not having sex with each other, but are stimulating themselves with inanimate objects. And someone saw it. That's very rock and roll.

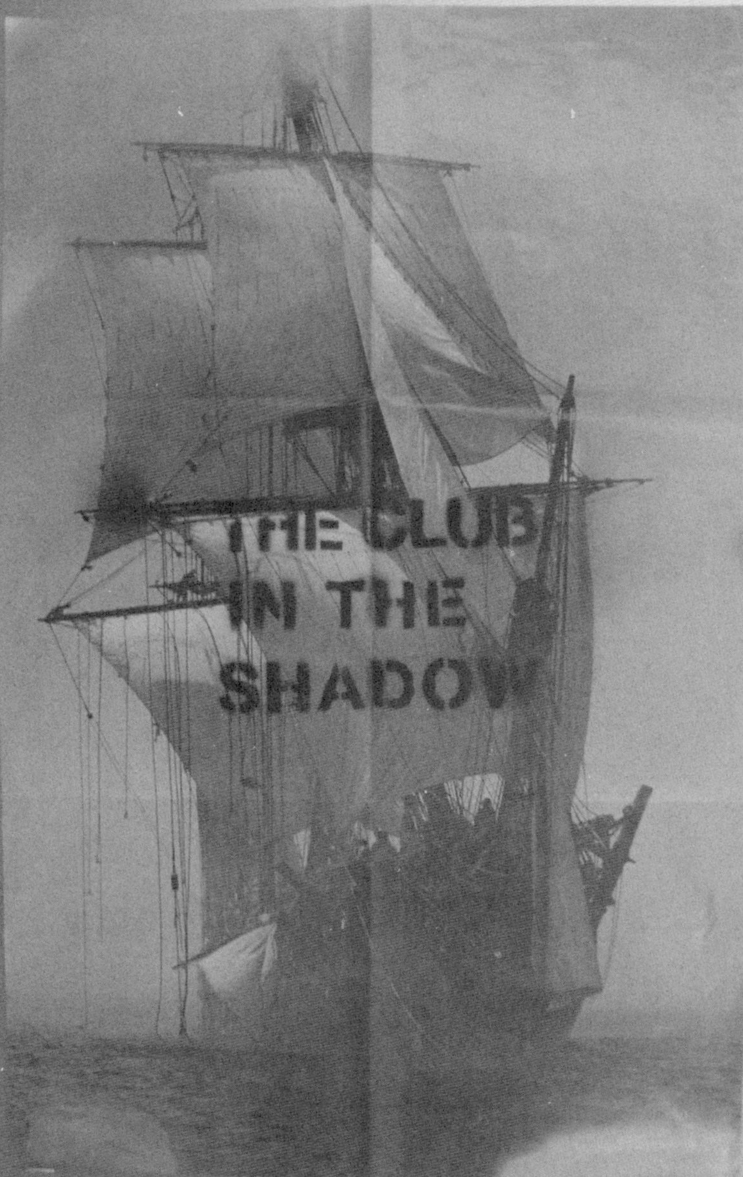
THE CLUB
IN THE
SHADOW

Classic Conceptual-Art Trouble
Kim Gordon and Jutta Koether in Conversation

Kim Gordon: When did you first start playing music? People always ask me that question.

Jutta Koether: So you're turning it on me? I don't know. You mean really going on stage?

KG: Yeah, like incorporating music into an art performance. When did you start doing more performative things?

JK: I think whatever I've done in music has come about through ideas about performance, rather than trying to be a musician or play music as such. I would probably date my first performance to a lecture-type thing I did with Diedrich Diederichsen and a literary writer in Munich in 1985 or '86. I had an acoustic guitar, but it functioned more like a symbol. I just played a little bit on it. But music, as integrated into the whole language of art and music interactions in New York, that was, I guess, with Rita Ackermann in 1997.

KG: That was straightforward music—eccentric music, but still in the realm of music.

JK: Yes, but in between all this is already another development in which I'm basically performing words with musical intermis-

Both long involved in art, music, and the crossovers between them, Kim Gordon and Jutta Koether have known and worked with each other for more than two decades. For this conversation, which took place in April 2013 in New York, they were asked to discuss the history of their interactions as well as the ideas that surrounded and motivated them.

Left: Kim Gordon and Jutta Koether, poster for "The Club in the Shadow," 2003

sions, or noise patterns—ideas of making musical inserts. Parallel to that are my more theoretical interests in music, music history, and music as a form of cultural expression. I don't know when that started. I think it started when I was a kid.

KG: You worked at *Spex* magazine.

JK: Yeah, but that was from the other side of things. Most of the musicians I dealt with at that time never tired of telling me I was the writer, I was not the practitioner. But through that experience I got interested in questions like "What is music?" or "What is musical expression in relation to other forms of cultural expression?" To me, they're all means of expression: music is one, talking is another, making paintings is yet another, and so on. How they meet and interact, and how they value one another—all these questions were interesting to me. In a way, that became my space of inquiry. If you're asking me to locate my interest in music, it's somewhere in that discursive field.

KG: There's also your interest in subgenres of popular music, like how punk rock figures into the culture, or goth, which seems to have much more of an influence in Germany …

JK: Really? I don't know …

KG: I don't know whether it's just playful, but you seem to think about it, even if it's just the playful use of certain goth elements in a performative manner.

JK: If you mean my collaboration with Steven Parrino in Electrophilia, I don't think that had much to do with goth.

KG: It had more to do with Kenneth Anger …

JK: … and with a more conceptual approach. There are certain extreme forms of appearance and staging in the history of rock culture, and if you don't belong to one—I never really genuinely *belonged* to a rock culture—it is interesting to put on a very particular costume that relates to it in some way. It's so distant that you can't really identify with it. You put it on as a performance, which makes it much more fun and much easier to use as a language. You're not burdened with having to do something truly meaningful, so it's this freeing element. You're liberated, in a way, from certain expectations. That's why underground cultures exist. They use certain things to become independent or at least to stage a certain idea of "freedom from," being "separate from," or being different. I can't speak for Parrino, but we had a lot of interesting discussions about these approaches, about why you choose certain aesthetic forms, about what different aesthetics mean, about what the formatting of your own body means when you act on a stage, and all sorts of other things. That's where we bonded. It just so happened that we chose a very rigid, very particular format of "black," with a certain surface appearance, a certain monolithic mode of playing, and a very strict set of rules. They linked up to an existing aesthetic language of, let's say, biker culture, or the American underground, or Kenneth Anger and such things. That aspect of it wasn't just a byproduct, but our main interest was in the more conceptual construct, not to play goth or something like that.

KG: I didn't mean to imply that you just "played goth." I meant that you utilized that type of stylized aesthetic. It says something a little more than punk rock, which kind of doesn't go anywhere at a certain point because, like goth, it's almost like a cartoon. But, like you've said, it also involves the aesthetics of black. Different aspects of it cross over into other cultural areas.

JK: Our interest was always more directed by aesthetic concerns in a larger sense than, say, youth culture or music culture. It was primarily a kind of art, that's all I'm saying.

KG: Is that why you sometimes wore masks while performing?

JK: Yes, in order to become part of a sculptural event. Not to be Jutta Koether, the artist, but almost literally to merge into the set, into a scenario of ideas, sounds, colors, and so on. To really break down the trappings of pop music, the burdens that ... well, that people like you have as pop stars, especially as a female. Maybe it's a kind of armor, but for all sorts of reasons I didn't want to go to that place. That's why I never sing. I speak, but there are never really vocals. My voice is not my instrument. It's just one tool out of many others. You have a very different way of entering the field of sounds, of making musical expression. All those decisions, on your part, they come from a history that's very different from mine.

KG: I *am* super aware that I'm playing on a stage. It's very hard to escape all of the expectations that people have for that sort of rock show, even if you're playing really unconventional music and don't really have any facility in conventional ways of playing an instrument. It's very hard to escape those trappings, as you put it, but it's similar to having a show in a gallery. A gallery is also a frame of expectations. How do you make something that's not just about an art object, but that's about the work or something else?

JK: But we were talking more about the artist. Do you think it's similar? When you show in a gallery, are all the expectations projected onto the artist's body like they are on a stage? I don't know.

KG: The work, rather than the artist's body, represents the artist, but the way it's lit and other aspects of display are, in a sense, the same as having a stage. I realize I'm straying a bit from your question. For me, music is much more of an area where ritual can happen, which is completely different from how I think about art making. It's something that I don't think successfully exists in art anymore. Music is very much about the spatial situation, and the body, and how the body affects sound, and movement affects sound, and how the audience is a willing partner in making it all come together. By agreeing to enter the space, the audience is almost confirming that what you're doing is music, or at least that it's a performance. It wouldn't be the same without an audience.

JK: There's a big difference between working with you and working with Parrino. With Parrino, it was almost the exact opposite. We were always rehearsing or—not rehearsing—we just called it playing. We basically did that privately, ritualistically, every week or every other week. The whole experience—going there, having a long conversation, making things together, thinking through artistic issues, playing the music, then going to dinner—it was like this one big thing, and playing music was just this one aspect within it. Only very occasionally did we venture out and play. On the other hand, the projects that you and I have done together, most of them really come to us from the outside. I'm invited to do something, and a gig, so to speak, becomes available, or vice versa. The decisions of how we will appear, what it looks like, how long we play, what is the content—all that is determined by the particular situation.

KG: It's based on context.

JK: Basically on the context, yes.

KG: When we did the show in Cologne using the famous Benjamin Buchloh interview of Gerhard Richter, it was almost like a play ...

JK: ... sort of a musical play. I played the Buchloh part, and you played Gerhard Richter. We were basically reading portions of the text, then inserting interludes where we tried to express or intervene into whatever we had said musically. That interview is, in a sense, a classic talk about what painting is supposed to mean, and so on, where they get into this kind of argumentative tone.

KG: But within that, we did set up a structure. It had a kind of ritualistic aspect to it as well.

JK: That's true. The interview already had an almost inherently ritualistic structure, because it resulted from the interaction of two people who have known each other forever, and you get the feeling this conversation has been enacted and reenacted by them many times throughout their lives. So our performance sort of weirdly picked up on the staged or ritualistic aspect of an argument that will never come to an agreement. That was the point, that there's always this dance between the two protagonists. That's also the nature of most of our collaborations: picking up on the context of the location, or the intentions of a given space, including our own intentions at a given moment if the performance relates to one of our individual exhibitions.

KG: With Parrino, it was like it was your band. You had a name, Electrophilia. It was your band. With Body/Head, Bill Nace and I also play together in our basement, and we have our own rituals. Body/Head is a bit weird, though, because people have a really hard time with the idea of improvisation. As though it's not any good, or it doesn't mean anything. But then, what Bill and I do doesn't necessarily come across as improvisation, either, because it seems sort of crafted since we play together so much and there are various elements that we repeat. But I still consider it music. It's not an art performance.

JK: Yes, but you've also chosen to be much more like a touring band. It's modeled much more after indie rock or experimental music.

KG: Eccentric noise music.

JK: Do you still relate it to your art projects? What relation does it have with your other work?

KG: It doesn't really relate so closely. Bill and I were showing other people's films behind us in slow motion, so I had Richard Kern come up and shoot some things that we could show behind us. But it's not going to look like art. It's just going to be another visual, something to look at.

JK: It's more like a backdrop.

KG: We think of the music as very filmic, somewhat like a film soundtrack, so I'm curious as to how the visuals will turn out. It definitely feels different when we play in a gallery or a non-conventional club. In a way, I prefer it, because then I feel like people have fewer expectations about what it's going to be. They know I'm not suddenly going to perform a Sonic Youth song. In the context of a gallery or a loft space, it feels more free, in a way. I feel more comfortable with it. An art audience is up for anything. It would be very different if you did the type of art performance you described in a club.

JK: I've done that. It feels weird, but I like it.

KG: It's interesting, right?

JK: My interest in such a situation is probably a little bit different than yours. For me, it has always been important to test these types of locations. What does it mean to fit something into a certain context? How can you, in a certain way, not fit? Or make the process of fitting in, itself, be felt by everybody in the room? How can you perform the awkwardness of being dislocated, of pushing one system into another? Things like that have always interested me. I've never functioned within the format of a professional musician, which is how your life has predominantly been shaped for quite a while now.

KG: For at least the last thirty years!

JK: That was another place where our interests met. Although you didn't come from the same place I came from, you also kept trying to test the limits, restrictions, and boundaries of the system that you grew into when you made the decision that you were part of a band, Sonic Youth. You went along with it, and that produced certain situations in which you then tried to figure out how to do something that, while still related, also tried to challenge that position. You didn't just stay there, but moved on into other fields, picking up other practices. I've always found it interesting to see how that has happened with you over the years in all of these different circumstances. Also, for me, it has been interesting to be dragged to a certain degree into your concerns and to think about design issues or the look of the body and other things.

KG: It's weird doing Body/Head with Bill when you get to a festival where the experimental tent is huge. Suddenly you realize that what we do doesn't fall easily into the category of noise music or even improvisation. It's something else again. So, it's also, in a way, not fitting in. It's challenging, but at the same time I'm not sure how healthy it is to be driven by not fitting in. Suddenly, you're confronted with questions like "How far can you take it? Can we make this popular?" There's always a question, for me.

JK: But what are you driven by, then?

KG: Well, I'm driven by more than one thing. I always have to decide which direction to go in. Is it going to go more into the art-world aspect, or is it just going to remain in a music context? It's just another form of expression. Doing work that's performative or has to do with traces of the body, that's where it meets up with my artwork. But there's no conceptual framework in the way there is in art practices. One of the appeals of seeing No Wave bands in New York early on was that it was such a strangely abstract music. It was very free and very abstract. If you didn't have any means to enter the galleries as an artist, being in a band was a way to be expressive and be independent of the gallery system. In art school I had been studying not just Conceptual art, but also Andy Warhol, and I was influenced by the Factory and Warhol's ideas about playing with popular culture. As well known as Warhol was, he still wasn't mainstream. The Factory's use of silver, spray-painting its interior silver, was something like a lo-fi design process. The films were also lo-fi. I was interested in the lo-fi quality of all of those activities. With the Factory, there was the glitz aspect, but it also had an almost seedy underbelly which I associated with lo-fi. In a way, the idea of playing in a band—the No Wave bands weren't mainstream—was associated with the idea of doing something with the subculture of the popular culture. Being part of a music culture or subculture appealed to me more than staying outside and commenting on it in a work of art.

JK: For me, in Germany, the idea of wanting to be involved in so-called pop culture, and the idea that it was different from the realm of high art had a lot to do with not having access. Popular music cultures, subcultural ideas, and the whole do-it-yourself or DIY aspect of early punk and proto-punk culture were appealing to me because they represented an alternative trajectory to that of the academy. Although I knew I wanted to be an artist, there was no door I knew how to open. Politically and socially the art scene was not ready for me, in a sense. So I thought, OK, you have to, so to speak, create your own terrain. In my case, that also came out of thinking through certain feminist issues like, "Who owns what? Who is in the museums? What do I want to look at? Where is the female voice or place?" And so on. I was trying to figure all that out as somebody who wanted to make art. At that time, music, music culture, writing about music, and the developments represented by or emerging out of early punk helped me establish this other cultural sphere. I've said this before, but my academy, so to speak, was *Spex*. It was a group of individuals—all coming from different places, whether it was studying politics, art, or philosophy, or being straight-ahead young music aficionados and wannabe journalists—forming an alliance. It was a very interesting formation in which I could function. That really set the agenda for my practice in the sense that there was always a range of possible activities, overlapping or operating in parallel, whether it be writing, or painting, or dealing with music, or any kind of performative action. Now, however, we are in a very different era where we have to deal with the fact that the liberating aspects of these DIY modes do not have the same effect anymore. They happened and have been used and cooped into something that is just one commodity among others.

KG: Producing kazillions of magazines that deal with fashion, art, and music under the umbrella of "culture." It's strange how much you take for granted clubs or venues or something like *Spex*, but they really do spawn little mini-eras where things come together, and suddenly they disappear. I can't imagine Sonic Youth starting out now and becoming what it became. What would that band be today? I don't know. Now that I'm focusing on art as a more central preoccupation, it's difficult. Although I've been doing it along the whole way, you think people won't take you seriously for doing art amidst all of the other stuff. Yet, at the same time I never really wanted a conventional art career, so I guess this is the art career that I wanted. My art academy was Dan Graham in the sense that he was someone who didn't just make work but who wrote about the cultural things that interested him, and at the time, he was very interested in music. He showed me that it wasn't enough to be in your studio making art that you were then just going to show in a gallery. You had to be part, not just of a painting dialogue, but of a more widespread and interesting cultural dialogue.

JK: Could you talk about how you experience the different cultural conditions of making art today? How that has changed for you over the past twenty years? Or has it?

KG: These are questions I wrestle with. I'm thinking about it, but I don't know if I have an answer yet. When I first started out with Design Office, it was also something to do because I didn't have access to a gallery. Like being in a band, it was a way to do something. I'm still interested in it and in picking up the thread by reexamining that work to find out what interested me about it, and making new work that relates to it but also to what I've been doing over the last twenty-five years or so. Design Office was a means to examine things psychologically in different circumstances, whether it was someone's apartment, a gallery, or an alternative space. Dan was a willing guinea pig in letting us intervene in his apartment. Another project was for an alternative space in Los Angeles called F.A.R. They didn't have a specific space; they staged things in different locations. I ordered them an ornate phone cover with their initials engraved in it so they could put it on different phones wherever they were. Another project was for White Columns when it was over on Spring Street. They were in an Art Deco-ish building, kind of like a showroom. I redid their office area, making it into something more like a dining room, because it was a community place. I put in a dining room table and redid the flooring. For the show I had there in 1981, I brought in chairs from different collector's houses. They were kind of hybrids of designs. They weren't like signature design chairs, they were more like second generation hybrids. When you and I did "The Club in the Shadow" at Kenny Schachter's gallery in 2003, we kind of approached it with similar ideas. What is the context? Well, the context was in part the location, which was below these two not-quite-completed Richard Meier towers surrounded at the bottom by a sort of rubble. People like Calvin Klein and Martha Stewart had already bought apartments, although they weren't living there yet, so we decided to make a club for the neighborhood.

JK: It was the beginning of the total gentrification of the West Side. Kenny Schachter had holed up in this small townhouse and had a permanent installation by Vito Acconci that was supposed to be the special attraction for his gallery. The whole thing was a ready-made disaster.

KG: It was a destination point and disaster. Nothing looked good there.

JK: Nothing looked good there because the gallery had a weird shape …

KG: … and the Acconci installation was made of metal fencing that you had to use hooks to hang things from.

JK: At the time, I was interested in the project as a way to join both of our interests. It was kind of an impossible, not re-designable design merged with the impossible desire of the gallerist to have something cool happening somewhere between music and art, a hunger for some kind of action. And Schachter himself was not considered a serious gallerist at the time, so you also have to consider the factor of his being some kind of underdog in the sphere of art dealers. So we were really in a very wobbly, strange, interstitial place, where we had to go in there and temporarily fulfill this fantasy for him, for ourselves, and for whomever else might come across it.

KG: It also had this upstairs. It reminded me of a '80s-style club, like Danceteria, where you would have a video lounge upstairs.

JK: We sort of redesigned the whole thing, and we put a program in there twice a week, mostly with very young artists. We, of course, didn't have a budget. It was all super lo-fi, and we recruited a lot of our friends and my students to do things.

KG: That's where Ei Arakawa did his first performance.

JK: It was his semester assignment instead of writing a paper! I said, "Hey, you gotta do something, because you haven't done anything all semester," so he designed a sequence of four performances. It was his first public appearance.

KG: No one really knew quite what was going on. For one of them, Ei handed pieces of paper with numbers on them to ten people or so and then just took them away. I don't know where they went.

JK: He took them around the block, literally in the shadows of these towers.

KG: It was at the end of this alley. It felt like the edge of Manhattan or something. And we had dancers. Every week we had different dancers.

JK: We made videos.

KG: But I remember, besides those, also Alan Licht playing …

JK: Oh, yes, we had dancing to noise music because we thought the club needed dance, to lend it some relation to Danceteria and movement. But people also just started to gather around …

KG: Just to hang out outside, sitting on the rubble around the tower. That was the best, seeing people sitting there drinking beer at the bottom of the Richard Meier towers.

JK: A few years later, based on this experience, we did it again, in a way, with us being more like the presenters and designers of a space when the Reena Spaulings gallery moved to East Broadway. For them, it was sort of a big shift going from a small place into this larger, loft-type space.

KG: It had certain characteristics.

JK: It had this character of being like a stage. Already, in a way, Reena was staging itself, or rather restaging itself as a "real" gallery, Reena Spaulings Fine Art. We sort of picked up on that and tried to really use what was then this newly inserted platform that takes up most of the space, and the notion of a dance floor or theatrical floor came out of that situation.

KG: Emily Sundblad saw it as something of a saloon. A salon or a saloon … it was like either/or. They wanted a piano and a bar.

JK: Again, we were really tapping into the hosts' desires as well as into the location.

KG: It used to be a bordello, I think, or a brothel upstairs.

JK: Well, there was this whole mythology of what the place had been. It had obviously been transformed many times, and residues of those transformations were visible in the layers of flooring with different patterns that you still see today in the front of the space. We sort of imported this whole idea of the stage and, again, dance.

KG: Also, there were these feminist shows that were starting to happen around, so we decided to make people really uncomfortable with notions of the body and dance. It was kind of influenced by the TV show *Deadwood*, the western, and the fact that most of the galleries we liked showed dead artists.

JK: We called the whole exhibition or series of events "Dead Already."

KG: And we had Ei build a corral. He was going to do this dance piece, and we gave him certain elements, like Dan Graham's recorded No Wave cassettes and …

JK: … and the pink, a body color …

KG: We got a carpet that was kind of a fleshy, kind of dusty pink body color that we put in the space. The floor was terrible, with nails sticking out, so we had to have something. We set up this corral that also worked as ballet bars or dance bars, and we also had some artwork.

JK: We had these dollies with stacks of art that kept being moved from one place to another depending on what was needed.

KG: We also had this series of events. One was an open dance class, an Isadora Duncan dance class. This woman who lives up in Northampton, Massachusetts. She came down with all of these tie-dyed silk tunics. It was supposed to be an open class hour before the actual performances started, but everyone showed up. Dan Graham was sitting in the front row watching.

JK: Joan Jonas, too.

KG: All these artists got into it. Everyone put on a tunic, and she led us in some class of Isadora Duncan dance. It was pretty funny.

JK: So that was, again, sort of a weird mixture of events, but also a merger of design, redesigning a space—literally redesigning it, but also tapping into some of the ideas about or behind the space—and trying to feed it something that was …

KG: … not quite right.

JK: They didn't know quite what to do with it. They wanted something like a relaunch or to reemerge from that move as something new. They were expecting this rebirth, but then we almost overloaded them with a string of activities and things that they didn't really ask for.

KG: It kind of set a precedent for everyone who comes to do shows at Reena Spaulings. They always make the gallery do stuff.

JK: In retrospect, it really acknowledged and initiated the whole idea of Reena being this different kind of place. Every subsequent artist does an "act" about Reena in that space, because of the way it looks, but also psychologically they're always doing something in relation to the "Reena Complex."

KG: There's some inner drama going on.

JK: It's not just another gallery. There's always this other layer, the Reena Complex, and you bump into it. In a way, our piece was really tapping into that condition.

KG: There's no documentation of it, which is really a shame. Just one shot of one of my paintings with a DVD on it.

JK: At the time, which was 2007, I think, we were both very present in the city and really able to recruit other people. Our activities kept bringing in new people, mainly in my case through students. Georgia Sagri and others who were still in school or just about to get out were in that dance piece. The whole enterprise represented some sort of collaborative mood that was going on at that time. It was around the time the Orchard gallery started to happen. People were really rethinking group activities. We had Karl Holmqvist reading poetry, Johanna Burton giving a lecture, and all kinds of things happening on the carpet that were not necessarily performance in the conventional sense, but giving an opportunity to do things.

KG: It's interesting just to create a situation where people come, and then it's something. It almost doesn't matter what's going on in the space. It has to be a certain element of not knowing exactly what's going to happen. Just when you think you're going to come back and see something that you know, it's different. Before that, we did the *Reverse Karaoke* tent for the "Her Noise" show in 2005. When I asked you to join in,

I already knew that I wanted to do *Reverse Karaoke*, but I thought it would be more interesting to make it into a "Club in the Shadow"-type project. They wanted to stage different events throughout the show, and I thought the tent could serve as a focal point, like a revival tent or something, for performances. And it was also just a huge space, so the idea was to have a tent that had its own space, that we painted.

JK: It has happened in our collaborations that, as in that case, you clearly imported me into that project. On other occasions, like the performance at the Moderna Museet in Stockholm in 2011, that was a larger show of my work, and I wanted our collaboration to be a part of it. Our performance there, the way we acted, was very particular to that space. We also did that other show in Graz, Austria, in 2009.

KG: Oh, right, oh my god! That was sensational. I really liked those pieces. It was supposed to be some kind of rock-music type of thing, but it wasn't supposed to be typical.

JK: The exhibition was called "Rock – Paper – Scissors." Diedrich Diederichsen curated it. It was art and music, artists who are trading in art and music at the same time.

KG: Like Red Krayola.

JK: … Albert Oehlen, Lucy McKenzie … a number of artists were in it.

KG: We had three of these vocal booths made out of foam-rubber soundproofing, which we used before in "The Club in the Shadow." Each one had a little video monitor of some noisy music, like this guy who lives up in Northampton and goes by the name Noise Nomads. I took it off YouTube. Another was Julie Cafritz singing the first song she ever wrote, which is basically just singing, "Fuck you, fuck you," or something like that. We annoyed people so much with that piece that they made us turn it around so the door didn't face the other installations. On the outsides of the booths we also had these paintings pinned with typical interview questions like "What's it like to be an icon?" or "What does music mean to you?" or "What's your favorite song?" Not many people commented on our work, but I liked it.

JK: I don't know what people made of it. It was definitely more of a situation of not trying to deliver. We did some other performance with heavy metal and Carly Simon lyrics too, but it somehow backfired. That happens. It's like classic conceptual-art trouble.

KG: "The Club in the Shadow" was the first real art project, but before that we did those paintings with Rita Ackermann for a show in Cologne.

JK: Three big ones! One was like a Georg Baselitz, one was like a Christopher Wool, and the third one was like a Philip Guston, and we hung them in the Museum Ludwig.

KG: I remember Rita saying her mother said, "These are the worst paintings you've ever done."

JK: I don't know what happened to them.

KG: I think they're in my basement. There was a flood, though, so I don't know what they look like now. At some point soon I'll have to open them up.

JK: They're probably nicely modified. Our collaborations have never really been spoken about or reviewed, but I think they were part of a fairly interesting cultural moment. That show at Reena Spaulings contributed something to a time that was, I think, really special.

KG: There were a lot of things going on then. There was, like you said, the collective project Orchard and also people's renewed interest in feminist art, like the big show "WACK! Art and the Feminist Revolution," which showed at the Brooklyn Museum.

JK: I think a new generation was looking for languages to expand their vocabulary into areas other than just making art and objects. It was also a time when the whole notion of performance really came back, like "full on" back, with the Performa performance biennial and so on. All these little things started to become visible again, which is why I find the idea of reintroducing dance really important. That came though your general interest in movement, as in "The Club in the Shadow," but also from being a singer on stage and using that as a means of expression and bringing that set of issues into the sphere of art.

KG: It had to do with dance and the body and things that might make John Kelsey really uncomfortable. But dance, I feel, had always been relegated to a sort of cultural ghetto. I've always looked to artists like Simone Forti, who were so influential.

JK: We wanted her to be in the Reena Spaulings project. It didn't work out, but we communicated with her, and she sent us the poem that became the poster. It was purple, and it had a kind of silver on it. It was done in this saloon-ish style: "Dead Already, presented by," and then our names, and then this poem.

KG: Do you have that? I'd really like to have that.

JK: It's still hanging at Reena Spaulings … in the bathroom!

KG: Oh, I'm going to go take it. Or at least take a picture of it.

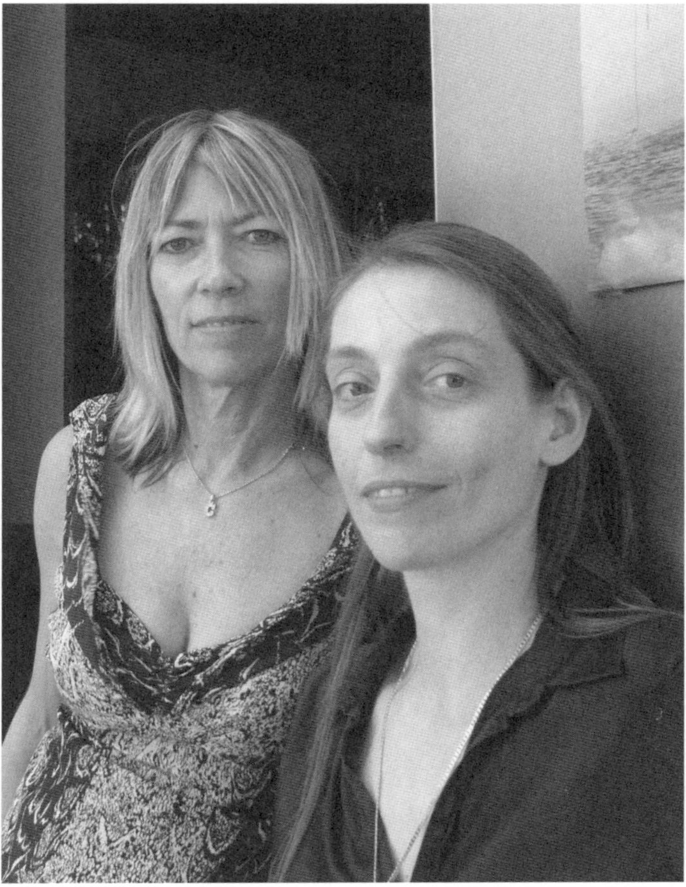

Kim Gordon is an artist, musician, writer, fashion designer, and actor. She is a founding member of the band Sonic Youth, formed in 1981 and on indefinite hiatus since 2011. In addition Gordon has recorded as part of the groups Free Kitten, Harry Crews, and Body/Head, as well as with musical collaborators including Ikue Mori, Yoko Ono, and Jim O'Rourke. Her writings have appeared in *Real Life*, *FILE*, *Artforum*, *Purple*, and *Texte zur Kunst*, among other publications. She has been exhibited at Reena Spaulings Fine Art, Gagosian Gallery, Kerry Schuss (KS Art), and Participant, Inc., while White Columns mounted "Design Office with Kim Gordon—since 1980" in 2013, a major survey of her visual art practice. Her memoirs are forthcoming from HarperCollins.

Jutta Koether is a painter, performance artist, musician, writer, and theorist. She is currently professor at the Hochschule für bildende Künste in Hamburg. Her work has been exhibited at the Whitney Museum of American Art, New York, Stockholm's Moderna Museet, Kölnischer Kunstverein, Akademie der bildenden Künste in Vienna, and Praxes, Berlin, among many other venues. Her writings have appeared in *Artforum*, *Flash Art*, *Artscribe*, *Texte zur Kunst*, and *Spex*, where she was a longtime editor and contributor. A founding member of the musical group Electrophilia with artist Steven Parrino, Koether has collaborated with Kim Gordon on a wide range of projects.

Branden W. Joseph is a professor of modern and contemporary art history at Columbia University and the author of four books, including *Beyond the Dream Syndicate: Tony Conrad and the Arts after Cage* (Zone, 2008). His writings on art, music, and film have appeared in *Artforum*, *Bookforum*, *Critical Inquiry*, *October*, *Parkett*, and *Texte zur Kunst*, as well as various exhibition catalogues.

8: Kim Gordon in New York, ca. 1975. Photo by Felipe Orrego. Courtesy of Felipe Orrego.

20: Kim Gordon, *Proposal for a Story*, 1977. Courtesy of Kim Gordon and White Columns.

26: Rhys Chatham, 1987. Photo: Catherine Ceresole. Courtesy of Catherine Ceresole.

28–29: Rhys Chatham (center) performing *Guitar Trio* with (left to right) Jules Baptiste, Wharton Tiers, and Robert Longo, ca. 1980. Photo: Debbie de Steffan. Courtesy of Rhys Chatham.

32: CKM members Kim Gordon, Christine Hahn, and Stanton Miranda at Massachusetts College of Art, 1980. Photographer unknown. Courtesy of Kim Gordon.

36: Frontispiece to "The Bedroom Displays Itself …" Originally published in *FILE*. Courtesy of Kim Gordon.

39: Dan Graham in his apartment after Design Office intervention, 1980. Originally published in *FILE*. Courtesy of Kim Gordon.

40: Photograph of copper-colored lamp from Design Office intervention, 1980. Originally published in *Real Life*. Courtesy of Kim Gordon.

44–45: Kim Gordon, *Men at Work*, as published in *Cave Canem*, 1982. Courtesy of Kim Gordon and John Miller.

46: Glenn Branca performing in Theoretical Girls at *X-Magazine* benefit, 1978. Photo: Gilles Bonnecarrère. Courtesy of Gilles Bonnecarrère and *Artforum*.

53: Laurie Anderson at the Institute of Contemporary Art, London, 1981. Photo: Chris Harris. Courtesy of the Institute of Contemporary Art, Philadelphia.

59: Glenn Branca performing *Symphony No. 2 (The Peak of the Sacred)* at St. Mark's Church, New York, 1982. Photo: Catherine Ceresole. Courtesy of Catherine Ceresole.

62: Robert Longo, cover drawing for Glenn Branca's LP *The Ascension*, 1981. Courtesy of Robert Longo.

69: Andy Warhol and Candy Darling in 1969. AP Photo. © 2014 The Associated Press.

73: Vito Acconci, *Conversions*, 1971. Enlargement from Super-8 film. Courtesy of Vito Acconci.

75: Kim Gordon, *Heroes*, ca. 1983. Courtesy of Kim Gordon and White Columns.

78–79: Jeff Wall, *Double Self-Portrait*, 1979. Color transparency in light box, 172 x 229 cm. Courtesy of the artist.

84, 87: Third Floor, Danceteria, New York City, undated. Photographer unknown. Courtesy of Kim Gordon.

88, 93: John Knight, *Project for Los Angeles Institute of Contemporary Art*, 1984. Installation view, Los Angeles Institute of Contemporary Art. Photo courtesy of John Knight.

96: Raymond Pettibon, untitled drawing from *Virgin Fears*, SST Publications, 1983. Courtesy of Raymond Pettibon.

99: Gram Parsons performing at Altamont Speedway, 1969. Photo by Robert Altman. Courtesy of Robert Altman.

105: Henry Rollins in Black Flag, 1980. Photo by Kerstin Rodgers/Redferns/ Getty Images.

107: Raymond Pettibon, *No Title (Did I do it? Do what?)*, 1987. Courtesy of Raymond Pettibon.

111: Mike Kelley, *If You Don't Want to Know the Definition Don't Open the Dictionary*, from the series "The Sublime," 1984. Courtesy of Mike Kelley Foundation for the Arts. © Estate of Mike Kelley.

113: Tony Oursler, *EVOL*, 1984. Enlargement from video. Courtesy of Tony Oursler.

116: Kim Gordon and Lee Ranaldo in Sonic Youth, 1986. Photo by Ebet Roberts/ Redferns/Getty Images.

130: Cover of *Fama & Fortune Bulletin*, 1991.

135: Tuesday Weld in a film still from *Cincinnati Kid*, 1965, as reproduced in *Fama & Fortune Bulletin*.

139: Tuesday Weld in a film still from *Bachelor Flat*, 1962, as reproduced in *Fama & Fortune Bulletin*.

143: Tuesday Weld in a film still from *Pretty Poison*, 1968, as reproduced in *Fama & Fortune Bulletin*.

146: Mike Kelley, *The Orange and Green* from *Pansy Metal/Clovered Hoof*, 1989. Courtesy of Mike Kelley Foundation for the Arts. © Estate of Mike Kelley.

150–51: Mike Kelley, *Ahh ... Youth!*, 1991. Courtesy of Mike Kelley Foundation for the Arts. © Estate of Mike Kelley.

154: Kim Gordon and Jutta Koether, poster for "The Club in the Shadow," 2003. Photo: Stefano Giovanni. Courtesy of Kim Gordon and White Columns.

177: Jutta Koether and Kim Gordon, 2003. Photo: Stefano Giovanni. Courtesy of Kim Gordon and White Columns.

Kim Gordon
Is It My Body? Selected Texts
Editor: Branden W. Joseph
Series editors: Isabelle Graw, Daniel Birnbaum, Institut für Kunstkritik,
Hochschule für Bildende Künste, Städelschule, Frankfurt am Main
Publisher: Sternberg Press

Managing editor: Max Bach
Proofreader: Niamh Dunphy
Design: Pascal Kress, Markus Weisbeck, Surface, Berlin/Frankfurt am Main

Printing: BUD Potsdam
Cover: Munken Print White 1.5 Vol, 300 gsm
Inside: Alster Werkdruck gelblichweiß, 1.5 Vol, 100 gsm
Typeface: Arno Pro; Akzidenz-Grotesk BQ
ISBN 978-3-95679-038-6

Sternberg Press
Caroline Schneider
Karl-Marx-Allee 78
D-10243 Berlin
www.sternberg-press.com